The Many Faces of Josephine Baker

OTHER BOOKS IN THE
WOMEN OF ACTION SERIES

■ ■ ■ ■

The Many Faces of
JOSEPHINE BAKER

DANCER, SINGER, ACTIVIST, SPY

Peggy Caravantes

CHICAGO
REVIEW
PRESS

Copyright © 2015 by Peggy Caravantes
All rights reserved
Published by Chicago Review Press, Incorporated
814 North Franklin Street
Chicago, Illinois 60610

ISBN 978-1-61373-034-8
Cover and interior design: Sarah Olson

Library of Congress Cataloging-in-Publication Data
    Caravantes, Peggy, 1935–
    The many faces of Josephine Baker : dancer, singer, activist, spy /
Peggy Caravantes.
        pages cm. — (Women of action)
    Summary: "Author Peggy Caravantes provides the first in-depth
portrait of Josephine Baker written for young adults. This lively biography
follows Baker's life from her childhood, to her participation in the civil
rights movement, her espionage work in WWII, and the adoption of
her twelve children. Also included are informative sidebars, fascinating
photographs, source notes, and a bibliography"-- Provided by publisher.
    Includes bibliographical references and index.
    ISBN 978-1-61373-034-8 (hardback)
    1. Baker, Josephine, 1906–1975—Juvenile literature. 2. Dancers—
France—Biography—Juvenile literature. 3. African American
entertainers—France—Biography—Juvenile literature. 4. Spies—
France—Biography—Juvenile literature. 5. World War, 1939–1945—Secret
service—France. I. Title.

    GV1785.B3C37 2015
    792.802'8092—dc23
    [B]
                                2014026074

Printed in the United States of America
5 4 3 2 1

Dedicated to friends, old and new

Contents

AUTHOR'S NOTE

RESEARCHING INFORMATION ABOUT Josephine Baker was a challenge because of the many versions of her life story. Most of the confusion is due to Josephine herself. She began to erase her early past when she left the United States for France at the age of 19. She destroyed every picture and paper she had because she did not want to remember those days of struggle.

Later on, when Josephine talked about her early life, her memories became more and more fanciful, more romantically embellished. No matter what time she was remembering, she was always aware of how it affected her public image at the moment she was speaking. She would say anything as long as she looked good in the story. Once, when challenged by a reporter about the truth of what she was saying, she responded heatedly that she did not lie—she just improved on life.

Her many biographers sorted through the myriad versions of her story, but they did not all reach the same conclusions. All of them consulted mounds of archival materials and interviewed hundreds of people who knew Josephine. Each biographer believed he or she had found the truth, and though there are many points upon which they agree, there are just as many on which they disagree. Consequently, depending upon a reader's choice of biography, the person will get only that writer's conclusions about what is truth about Josephine Baker.

In the process of trying to sort it all out, a lot of misinformation has been repeated by writer after writer. But the truth is nebulous—almost impossible to pin down. I'm not sure that, by the end of her life, Josephine *herself* could separate fact from fiction.

I, too, have struggled while searching through many resources, trying to distinguish truth from fabrication. My goal has always been to introduce today's young readers to the story of a remarkable woman who rose from poverty, overcame racial prejudice, and became a star, even as she remained an enigma.

The Many Faces of Josephine Baker

Her Own Journey

WITH ONLY THE CLOTHES ON HER BACK, 13-year-old Josephine Baker, along with Clara Smith and the Dixie Steppers, climbed aboard a train headed for Memphis, Tennessee. As the train moved through East St. Louis, Illinois—one of America's worst slums, filled with dilapidated and sordid housing—Josephine pressed her nose against the car's window. Dense clouds of coal smoke mixed with the stench of dying cattle. Piles of garbage filled the overcrowded streets. Remembering her years there, Josephine vowed: "I'm leaving here a nobody but someday I'm gonna be somebody . . . and you ain't gonna get to see me . . . 'cause I ain't ever coming back here again!"

And so began Josephine Baker's journey to fulfill her dream of becoming a star.

Born Freda Josephine McDonald on June 3, 1906, in the St. Louis Female Hospital, she was the daughter of Carrie McDonald, a washerwoman, and Eddie Carson, a drummer in St. Louis gambling houses. The two dated, and about a year after they met, Carrie gave birth to Josephine. The round, roly-poly infant reminded her of Humpty Dumpty. When Carrie had first heard the egg's name said aloud, the words sounded like "Tumpy." That became the nickname that stayed with Josephine throughout her childhood.

Carrie became pregnant again when Josephine was 16 months old. With the birth of Richard Alexander on October 12, 1907, the happy-go-lucky Eddie deserted Carrie, leaving her to provide for the babies. She struggled for a couple of years to earn enough money to keep the household running, but she was unsuccessful. Eventually, she married 23-year-old Arthur Martin, a brawny factory worker, thinking he would provide for her and the two children. Unfortunately, his moodiness and quick temper often cost him jobs, so Carrie took in laundry to support the family.

For the next several years, the family of four lived in a succession of run-down, rat-infested dwellings. Josephine's stepfather often failed to pay the rent. Each time a landlord evicted the family, they searched for another place to live. The financial situation grew worse with the births of two more girls, Margaret and Willie Mae. The hard life discouraged Carrie. She often took out her frustration on her oldest daughter, who resembled the father who had deserted them. In later years Josephine recalled, "Mama said things to me I'm sure she couldn't mean, that she hated me and wished I were dead."

At age six, Josephine attended first grade at Lincoln Elementary School, which served poor and middle-income black students. Her only school clothing was a blue dress trimmed in white, and she wore it every day for the entire year. The other children mocked her lack of shoes. To get them to laugh about something else, Josephine became the class clown. She crossed her eyes, stuck out her tongue, and made silly faces. Mostly, she wanted to get out of the overcrowded classroom of 50 students and be free to roam the streets of her neighborhood. In the next few years, Josephine attended school only about one day in three; she didn't learn to read and write until adulthood.

During part of her first-grade year, Josephine stayed with her Grandma McDonald and Aunt Elvira, who lived in the same neighborhood. Elvira, who headed the family, was a large copper-skinned Cherokee woman with a booming voice and two braids of long black hair. She spent her time either weaving shawls or performing tribal dances in the house. The loud sounds she made when dancing scared Josephine, who always ran outside. In contrast, Josephine enjoyed being with her grandmother, who showed her the love for which she longed. She baked cookies and cornbread for the little girl and told her stories about her great-great grandparents who were slaves brought from Africa to America. She sang to her, told her Bible stories, and repeated over and over Josephine's favorite story, *Cinderella*.

Josephine wished she could be like Cinderella and change from her dirty, tattered clothes into beautiful gowns with sparkling jewels. She created a fantasy world and acted it out in the basement of her grandmother's house. From some of Mrs. McDonald's old clothes, Josephine created costumes for the plays she performed for the neighborhood children. She made benches for her audience by placing boards across boxes. She charged each person a penny to watch her sing and dance. As part of the performance and to get the laughter she craved, Josephine crossed her eyes and grinned broadly—techniques she used in show business as she grew older.

One Sunday, Josephine was walking from church to her grandmother's house when she stepped on a rusty nail that punctured her bare foot. It became infected, and her leg swelled to an alarming size. Her foot was so painful that her mother took her to the hospital, where the doctor wanted to amputate the leg. Josephine became hysterical at the thought of never walking or dancing again.

"No! No! Please don't cut if off," she shrieked. The doctor agreed to drain the wound first. Ugly, smelly, infected blood oozed out, but the technique saved her leg.

After leaving the hospital, Josephine returned to live with her parents and her siblings. Another child to feed increased the family's money problems. After Josephine's leg healed, Carrie told her that because she was the oldest child, she must earn money to help support them. At first seven-year-old Josephine went around the neighborhood looking for jobs. She offered to sweep steps or clean snow from sidewalks. Few people hired her. Then Carrie found her daughter a job as a maid for a widow named Mrs. Kaiser. In exchange for the child's work, the woman would provide her clothing and food. With that job, Josephine's childhood ended.

For a short time, Mrs. Kaiser was good-hearted to the young girl; she bought Josephine a dress and a pair of shoes. But the kindness didn't last long: the widow was a bully and began treating Josephine like a slave. The little girl worked hard at the woman's large country house, but because of Missouri's compulsory education law, she also had to attend school. So Josephine rose each day at 5 AM in order to complete all her tasks as a maid before going to school. For breakfast she ate cold potatoes and then carried coal, lit a fire in each room, chopped wood, scrubbed steps, and swept the rooms. She returned from school to peel potatoes, wash dishes, clean the kitchen, and do laundry. For supper, the woman provided the child cold cornbread and molasses, which Josephine shared with a white rooster she named Tiny Tim.

When Josephine's chores ended around 10 PM, she picked up Tiny Tim and stumbled to the cellar. There, she slept in a wooden box with the dog, Three Legs, who gave her fleas. She scratched and scratched. Her scratching annoyed Mrs. Kaiser, who beat the child to make her stop, but first the widow made the girl remove her clothes so that the blows would not wear out the fabric. As Tiny Tim grew fatter from sharing Josephine's pitiful dinners, Mrs. Kaiser began eying him as a potential meal for herself. One day, she told Josephine to kill Tiny Tim so he could be prepared to eat. With tears streaming down her cheeks, the child grabbed the bird between her legs and cut its neck with a pair of scissors. The squawking and the warm blood covering her hands traumatized Josephine. She wanted to run away but knew it would be useless because she was so young and had nowhere to go.

Exhaustion, lack of food, and fear took their toll on the child. She became thinner and thinner and developed a rasping cough. One day, she felt especially ill and forgot to watch the water she was boiling to wash dishes. Some of it splashed over on the stove. Mrs. Kaiser grabbed one of the girl's hands and plunged it into the pot of boiling water. Josephine later described what happened next: "I scream, I scream, Mother, Mother, help me. I escape to the next house screaming like a lunatic. I fall in front of the door. All my skin and my fingernails are boiled, ready to fall off. The blood is cooked. When I wake up, I'm in the hospital."

Carrie had to take Josephine home again, but not for long. She soon found another household to employ her daughter. In early January, Josephine went to work for the Masons, a childless couple. They agreed to provide a room and food in exchange for the girl's housework in their beautiful home. The Masons treated Josephine kindly. They provided her with a real bed and enough nourishing food that she gained weight. They allowed her to play with the neighborhood children and to attend school, wearing pretty clothes and shoes that Mrs. Mason bought her.

In their basement, Josephine used worn velvet curtains to set up a theater. Mrs. Mason gave her old clothes and a feathered hat to wear as costumes. She entertained the children in the neighborhood by singing and dancing for them. For the first time in a long time, Josephine felt happy. But her contentment did not last.

For several nights she heard a noise like heavy breathing and thought a ghost had come to her room. She told Mrs. Mason about the sounds. Her employer told her that if the phantom came back, Josephine should call her. That night she heard it again. When the ghost tried to climb into her bed, Josephine yelled, "Oh, it's the ghost, Mrs. Mason, please come quick!"

The woman rushed to the little girl's room and discovered that the ghost was Mr. Mason.

The next morning, Mrs. Mason told Josephine she could not work for the couple anymore. Josephine did not understand why she had to leave and thought the woman was angry because she had been scared. She promised not to yell out again, but her employer did not relent. Josephine asked if she could take her new clothes with her. Mrs. Mason agreed. When Josephine went to the basement to collect them she realized, "Never again would I draw back the musty velvet curtains. Never again would I wear my feathered hat. I would never again be queen. I choked back my tears. Somewhere deep inside me I vowed that somehow I would grow up to be a famous star with beautiful flowing gowns."

Josephine returned home, where Carrie blamed her daughter for losing a good job. The money was more important to her than her daughter's safety, and she ignored what would have happened to Josephine if she had remained in the Mason household. Josephine's stepfather, Arthur, just laughed at the child's naiveté.

These two experiences of working in someone's home scared Josephine. At not quite eight years old, she decided to find her own work and gathered a group of neighborhood children who also needed to earn money. They walked to the part of town where white families lived and sought work there. The children offered to scrub or wax floors, polish furniture, run errands, shovel snow, and babysit. Josephine's height and slender frame made her look older, and she claimed to be 15 years old. She told potential employers that she was stronger than she looked. For each job she got, she made about 50 cents. She kept a nickel for herself and gave the rest to Carrie for the family. When they could not get jobs, Josephine and the other children rummaged through white people's garbage, looking for a chicken neck or fish head or a few discarded vegetables to make soup.

In another attempt to earn a little money, Josephine and her siblings often went to the Union railroad yard, where they picked up lumps of coal and stuffed them in sacks. They later sold the coal pieces for a few pennies each. Josephine became daring enough to leave her brother and sisters on the ground and climb on top of hopper cars. From there, she threw them larger pieces of coal that sold for more money. Pushing the limits, she jumped down only when she felt the rumble of the train starting to move. She recalled, "I throw myself. The train just accelerating . . . I fall on the ground."

Josephine spent any spare time visiting her grandmother and her aunt, who one day invited the young girl to come live with them again. Josephine agreed. She was no longer scared of her Aunt Elvira, who didn't seem as big as she remembered. Elvira spoke more softly and acted tired. At her grandmother and aunt's house, Josephine had her own bed instead of having to sleep on the same bedbug-infested mattress with her three siblings.

Josephine had lived with her relatives only a short time when, in the middle of the night, her grandma awoke Josephine. A frantic Mrs. McDonald told her granddaughter to go get Carrie because Elvira was dying. For many years, Elvira had suffered from a heart disease known as chronic endocarditis. Josephine rushed down the street to get her mother, but by the time they returned, Elvira had died. She left Grandma McDonald a small pension, and the older woman went to live with Josephine's family. The extra money improved the financial situation somewhat, and they moved into a one-room shack in Boxcar Town in East St. Louis.

Holes riddled the hovel where Josephine and her family lived. In the places where floorboards didn't meet, they hammered flattened chili and tomato tin cans over the holes to keep out the swarms of rats. They plugged the cracks in the walls with old newspapers and magazine pages. Josephine tried to improve the place by planting some geraniums in a little garden in front of the house, but they never had a chance to come up. At night, in chilly weather, Josephine covered herself with a thin, worn patchwork quilt and cuddled two black-and-white puppies she had found searching through garbage cans for food. She nurtured the little strays by feeding them stale bread dipped in milk.

A scary incident one night in July 1917 caused Josephine to recall what her grandma told her when Elvira died. Josephine had been scared to look at the dead body, but her grandma said there was more to fear from the living than from the dead. Josephine learned the truth of that statement when mobs of armed white people invaded Boxcar Town and attacked its inhabitants. Upon hearing the screams and gunshots, Carrie woke 11-year-old Josephine by jerking the threadbare quilt off her. The shivering, frightened girl struggled to get dressed. She and the family

EAST ST. LOUIS AND BOXCAR TOWN

Boxcar Town—located in East St. Louis, Illinois, across the Mississippi River from St. Louis, Missouri—was one of the worst slums in the United States in 1917. The name came from the fact that most of the "houses" were, in fact, abandoned boxcars. The residents were black people who had moved north to work during World War I. When white union workers at the Aluminum Ore Company and the American Steel & Wire Company went on strike, the factories hired black workers as strike breakers. Racial tension grew.

On July 2, 1917, a mob of about 25 white people attacked every black person they encountered. Large crowds encouraged the rioters, who set 200 boxcars and shacks on fire. As the black men, women, and children ran from their burning homes, white mob members clubbed them, shot them, and even lynched a few. The reported number of fatalities varied from 48 to 200. That night almost 7,000 black residents fled across the Mississippi River to St. Louis, Missouri, and most never returned.

raced out of their shanty just as a lighted torch sailed through a window. They huddled in the darkness behind trees and bushes. Throughout the whole ordeal, Josephine refused to let go of her puppies.

By morning, the massacre had ended, leaving most of the black community homeless. All that remained of Boxcar Town was smoke and ashes. The victims had no homes, and no possessions. Following the riots, Josephine's family moved from tenement to tenement. Carrie took in laundry for both black and white people. Josephine resented having to scrub other people's clothes over rough washboards and having to ride the trolley to deliver the laundry to various neighborhoods. Sometimes her black clients could not pay her—not because they did not want to, but because they had no money. Josephine often returned home with a couple of dollars instead of the $20 she should have collected. Since they could not pay for Carrie's labor, some of the black women offered to help her by carrying water for her, cleaning her house, or sending food.

Yearning to escape the hard work and harshness of her life, Josephine became a waitress at the Old Chauffeur's Club, a hangout for jazz musicians. She waited on customers and washed dishes for $3 a week. Although she still worked hard, she preferred these tasks to doing laundry. In the evenings, Josephine attended neighborhood dances. At one of these, she met Willie Wells, a 25-year-old steelworker. Before long, he asked her to marry him. Josephine had no experience with men, but she wanted to get out of her house. Although Josephine accepted Willie's proposal, Carrie had to approve the marriage since her daughter was only 13, and underage. However, the union was never legal because Missouri had a minimum age of 15 to marry, even with parental approval.

On December 11, 1919, Josephine and Willie took their vows in a traditional wedding attended by family and friends in a neighborhood Baptist church. The bride wore a simple wedding gown provided by an aunt, and the groom dressed in a suit. At the conclusion of the ceremony, everyone went to Carrie's home for a meal of roast pork and baked macaroni. That night the newlyweds moved into a rented furnished room upstairs.

After the wedding, Josephine did not work but rather played the role of housewife, although she found it boring. Within a couple of months, she started to knit baby clothes. She told no one that she was pregnant but did purchase a wooden bassinet. Willie was not a good financial provider, and the couple often had trouble paying the $1.50 per week rent. One night the couple had a loud argument, and Willie became violent. Josephine grabbed a bottle, shattered it against the table, and struck Willie. Wounded, with a deep cut over one eye and blood streaming down his face, he dashed out of the room, never to return again.

Josephine stopped knitting baby clothes. No one ever knew whether she had really been pregnant or whether she had miscarried. As though the marriage had never occurred, she went back to her old job as a waitress at the Old Chauffeur's Club, and she hoped to soon find a way to leave not just her home life, but St. Louis itself.

In her free time, Josephine visited her neighbors, the Joneses, a group of traveling musicians. The mother, Dyer, an outstanding trumpeter, taught Josephine to play the trombone. The family invited her to go with them as they roamed up and down the neighborhood streets singing, stomping their feet, and dancing. Carrie either didn't know or didn't care that her daughter missed school to perform with the Joneses.

On Sunday afternoons, Josephine attended shows at the Booker T. Washington Theater, which featured black entertainers. She saw the show of a vaudeville group called the Dixie Steppers so many times that she memorized every line of dialogue and every movement of the chorus dancers. She wanted to perform on that stage and told her nine-year-old sister Margaret, "I'm going to talk to the director. Since we're going to have to work someplace, why not in show business? Wouldn't that be fun?" Margaret ignored her sister because she didn't believe the director would speak to her, let alone hire her.

But Josephine was determined. First, she convinced the stage-door guard she had an interview, and he let her in. Josephine waited her turn to be called onstage, but the director ignored her. Finally, as the rehearsal ended, he told her to come back the next day. A few minutes later, Josephine rushed back to her sister: "It worked! I'm hired!"

The following morning, he ordered her onstage and told her to join the chorus line. The music began, and Josephine started to dance the memorized steps. Slowly her body responded to the music. She moved in such a supple, limber manner and with such boundless energy that the other girls laughed. The director stopped the music, and Josephine waited to be fired. Instead he announced he was giving her the role of Cupid in their vaudeville production of Shakespeare's *Romeo and Juliet*. He instructed her to report for rehearsals the next day. Although Josephine was thrilled, she did not tell her mother about the play because she knew Carrie would object to her wearing the revealing costume. Only her sister Margaret knew that Josephine planned to make her stage debut at the tender age of 13.

In her role as Cupid, Josephine dressed in pink tights and a skimpy costume with pink wings attached. Fastened in a harness and suspended by a rope from the ceiling, she performed well in the role until the wings got stuck in part of the backdrop. The more she fought to free herself, the more entangled she became. Below her on the stage, actors playing Romeo and Juliet waited for Cupid to shoot them with a love arrow. Instead Josephine floated in circles above them, flailing her arms, acting like an unstrung marionette. The audience erupted in laughter. Josephine was embarrassed. She wished the curtain would come down so she could free herself, and she figured her acting career was over. But the director heard members of the audience talking about how much they loved that day's show. Instead of firing her, the director told Josephine to keep her performance the same. She couldn't believe her luck.

One Sunday, Josephine studied the posters at the Booker T. Washington Theater. She noticed an announcement of the performance of Clara Smith, a noted African American blues singer. Josephine paid the 25¢ admission fee and entered the darkened theater, where she found a seat in the first row to watch the play unfold before her. With her eyes focused on the stage, especially on the long silk scarf Clara Smith used as a prop, Josephine sat motionless until the show ended and the curtain came down.

VAUDEVILLE

Vaudeville was a type of light entertainment popular in the United States from the mid-1890s until the early 1930s. During that time, more than 25,000 performers took to the vaudeville stage, making it the most popular form of American entertainment. Traveling shows consisted of 10 to 15 short, unrelated acts that might include comedians, singers, dancers, musicians, acrobats, ventriloquists, plate-spinners, and any other act that could entertain an audience. Because vaudeville not only amused but also presented a cross-section of the cultural diversity in America at that time, it became the earliest form of entertainment to cross racial and class boundaries.

Then she sneaked backstage, where she found Clara Smith. She noticed the singer had spilled food on her white costume. Josephine offered to clean the clothing. The singer agreed and removed the dress. Josephine found water, washed the dress, and then pressed it between towels to dry it. Within a couple of hours, she returned the costume free of all stains. Clara paid her a dollar.

As Josephine rejoiced over having that much money, Clara surprised her further by inviting Josephine to travel with her as her dresser. She offered to pay Josephine's train fare wherever they went plus $10 a week as salary. Josephine thought about the offer for a minute. She knew the Jones Family Band had joined the vaudeville troupe, so she would know someone. The Dixie Steppers would go too. Plus, she could finally escape from St. Louis. Without hesitating any longer, she accepted.

Josephine didn't go home that night, but she did share her plans with her sister. "Margaret, before I say another word I want you to cross your heart. Good. Now swear that you won't tell Mama—I'm leaving town tomorrow with the show."

Even though she was brokenhearted at the thought of her big sister going away, Margaret covered for her that night. She said Josephine was spending the night with the Jones family. The next day when her older daughter still did not come home, Carrie questioned Margaret again. Finally, she told her mother that Josephine had left on a train with Clara Smith. With no emotion, Carrie said, "She has chosen her path. Let her be."

2

Show Business Debut

ONE NIGHT, JUST 15 MINUTES BEFORE the show opened for its last stop in Philadelphia, a chorus girl fell and hurt her knee. Josephine saw her chance to perform onstage. She begged the director to let her replace the injured girl, assuring him she knew all the steps. With the minutes ticking away, he had no choice and told her to put on the costume. Josephine scrambled to get ready. The short skirt was too big and slid down to mid-calf instead of above her knees. The black tights wrinkled on her skinny legs and pooled around her ankles.

When she appeared onstage at the end of the chorus line, the audience took one look at her baggy clothing and roared with laughter. Josephine enjoyed making people laugh and began a clown-like performance. She acted clumsy, stuck out her tongue, and crossed her eyes while a stupid grin spread across her face. At school in St. Louis, she had received reprimands for these same actions. Now she used them to entertain the audience. She commented, "Seeing everybody looking at me electrified me."

At the end of that night's performance, the director, Bob Russell, told her that he wanted her to do exactly what she had done that night at every performance. At last Josephine was performing onstage, but she was not satisfied. She wanted to dance like the rest of the chorus instead of being the funny girl. Before she could achieve that goal, the show closed. Most of the performers went home, but a woman named Sandy Burns put together a dance show and invited Josephine to again perform at the end of the chorus line. She accepted the temporary job.

When she wasn't onstage, Josephine spent her time with the leading lady, Clara Smith, whose unusual appearance fascinated the young girl. The short and fat black woman sported a red wig worn with paper flowers or a huge bow. The purple powder she spread across her face contrasted sharply with her teeth, yellowed by years of pipe smoking. Her favorite outfit was a short gauzy dress worn over pink tights, with her feet encased in high heels. In return for taking care of her whenever she had eaten too much sweet potato pie, the actress gave Josephine an alphabet book so that she could start learning to write her letters.

When they traveled, the black performers could not stay in white hotels because of segregation. There were few hotels for blacks because there were not enough blacks who needed that service. The performers had to stay in boardinghouses, where several women shared rooms and beds. Maude Russell, a black dancer and singer who often performed on the same stage with Josephine, explained the situation this way: "Many of us had been kind of abused by producers, directors, leading men. . . . And girls needed tenderness, so we had girl friendships, the famous lady lovers, but lesbians weren't well accepted in show business. . . . I guess we were bisexual, is what you would call it today."

As they traveled together, Josephine and Clara Smith became lovers. Josephine's sexual interest in women did not stop when, in later years, she was able to afford her own room. She continued to have female lovers throughout her life, in addition to her relationships with men.

In the evenings, Josephine attended neighborhood parties. At one of them she met 23-year-old William "Willie" Howard Baker, a small, wiry, African American man with a light complexion. The two were attracted to each other because of their shared love of dancing. Josephine's youth and her fun-loving nature also appealed to him. When he smiled at Josephine and invited her to dance, she said yes. They got to know each other better, and Josephine learned that Willie, a former jockey, now worked as a porter on Pullman cars. His charming personality and his steady job impressed her. After a few months, Willie proposed, and she accepted. Although Josephine was 15, legally old enough to wed at that time, they encountered problems getting a marriage certificate in Philadelphia.

PULLMAN PORTERS

Pullman cars were railroad sleeping cars built and operated by the Pullman Palace Car Company for about 100 years from the mid-1860s to the 1960s. Pullman porters were men who worked on these cars. Thousands of black men took the jobs, and by the 1920s, the Pullman Company was the largest single employer of black men in the country.

Porters converted seats into berths in the evening and reversed the process the next morning.

(continued on the next page)

They assisted passengers with luggage and performed other requests, such as brushing a coat or suit, or polishing shoes. Although they received better wages than most black men of their time, porters' salary of $810 a year in 1926 (equal to $7,500 today) was extremely low payment for the 400 hours they worked each month. Porters also had to pay for their own meals and supply their own uniforms and shoe polish. To their friends and neighbors, however, the Pullman porter held a respected position that offered him a steady income, a chance to travel across America, and little of the heavy physical labor associated with most jobs for black men in the late 19th century.

Their difficulty in obtaining a marriage license plus the objections of Willie's parents to the marriage caused the couple to elope. After the show in which Josephine was performing closed, she and Willie traveled to Camden, New Jersey, where a justice of the peace performed the marriage ceremony. Josephine no longer carried the McDonald surname with which she associated her unhappy childhood in St. Louis. She was now Josephine Baker—the name she used the rest of her life—despite two other later marriages.

The couple lived with Willie's parents in a tense relationship. Willie's mother did not like her new dark-skinned daughter-in-law. Josephine told a friend, "If somebody came to the house, Willie's mother would find some excuse to keep me in the kitchen."

It was ironic that the Bakers considered her too dark; growing up Josephine had always felt out of place in her family because her skin was so much lighter than that of her siblings and her mother.

Willie's father owned a restaurant, and the young couple ate there most of the time. They got to know people who frequented the restaurant, and Josephine became friends with Wilsa Caldwell, who later helped her out in New York City.

Unlike the first time she lived with a man, Josephine did not become a housewife. Instead she sought out other performing jobs. One day she heard about *Shuffle Along*, a new black musical coming to Philadelphia. As the group passed through various cities, they held one-night auditions to allow aspiring chorus dancers to try out. The show's goal was to open in New York City, and Josephine was determined to be with them when they performed on Broadway.

In April 1921, at the Dunbar Theatre in Philadelphia, a nervous Josephine auditioned for the fast-paced musical before two of the producers, Noble Sissle and Eubie Blake. When her dance ended, she heard the men discussing her. Words like "too thin," "too small," and "too dark" reached her ears moments before they announced their verdict: no role for Josephine in *Shuffle Along*. She did not know she never had a chance of being hired because the law required a chorus girl to be 16 years old to perform onstage. Failure to make the cast crushed Josephine. As her eyes filled with tears and her head drooped, she stumbled down the steps leading to the stage door exit. Her sobs echoed as she burst out the door and disappeared into the rain.

Undeterred, Josephine followed the show's progress and learned that *Shuffle Along* had opened in New York City. They were not on Broadway but in an old, dilapidated vaudeville theater called 63rd Street Music Hall. Still wanting a job in that show, Josephine decided to follow them to New York. She left her husband, Willie Baker, to whom she never returned, and, with the few dollars she had saved, bought a one-way train ticket for the 90-mile trip to the big city.

The only person Josephine knew in New York City was Wilsa Caldwell, the casual friend she had met at her father-in-law's restaurant. Wilsa danced in the *Shuffle Along* chorus line, and Josephine decided to look for her at the theater since she did not know her friend's home address. Josephine slept two nights on benches in Central Park until she located the 63rd Street Music Hall. Eventually she found Wilsa, who told her the show had been so successful in New York that the producers were gathering a separate troupe to perform the show on the road. She encouraged Josephine to try out for that show. Recalling the remark at her previous audition that she was too dark-skinned, Josephine covered her face and body with light powder before she went onstage to audition for Al Mayer, another of the show's producers. Mayer wasn't aware of his partners' earlier rejection of Josephine, so he hired her for the road show chorus line at a salary of $30 per week. He apparently also didn't know that she was still not 16, the minimum age for a chorus girl.

The show opened in Chicago, and Josephine once again found herself at the end of the chorus line—in the comic position. She took advantage of the opportunities in this role and tripped over her own feet, crossed her eyes, stuck her tongue in her cheek, and folded her knees together in a froglike position.

Despite acting the clown, she managed to maintain the rhythm of the music. The audience loved her, but the rest of the chorus hated her because she detracted from their performance. They were the stars, not Josephine. To get even, they tripped her as she came onstage. She turned the stumble into another comic act. Some of the girls moved all of her possessions out of their shared dressing room and dumped them in the hall. She did not let this stop her—she changed costumes in the restroom.

In 1925 Josephine Baker hams it up for the king of French fashion, Paul Poirot, who later designed many of her clothes.

© *Underwood & Underwood/Corbis*

The New York version of the show closed in July 1922, and Sissle and Blake decided to take the original cast on the road. However, they had heard that one of the dancers in the previous road show was popular. They learned that it was Josephine and invited her to join the regular troupe. The cast left New York on July 15 and headed to Boston and other major United States cities—including St. Louis. When Josephine heard that the show would visit her old hometown, she tried to write a note to her mother, but she had difficulty spelling even simple words because she had seldom attended school.

When they arrived in St. Louis, Josephine visited her family in their basement room in the old neighborhood. She was shocked by the conditions in which they lived. "I had grown used to electricity and a bathroom, and here I was with a kerosene lamp, a bucket and dipper, and a communal washtub. There were dirty dishes under the bed. . . . I was ashamed of my own mother." Just a short time before, Josephine would have accepted the situation as normal.

Happy to see their sister, Richard, Margaret, and Willie Mae begged her to tell them stories about life in show business. Josephine was saddened to discover that 11-year-old Willie Mae had lost sight in one eye when a dog clawed her. Josephine wanted a better life for her younger sister and promised to send $50 a month for Willie Mae's clothing and education. She told her brother and sisters that she would come back to see them at Christmas, but she didn't. In fact, 14 years passed before Josephine saw her family again. Each year, though, she continued to send more and more money for the family.

Meanwhile, because of the success of *Shuffle Along*, Sissle and Blake created a new show, *In Bamville*, into which they wrote a special part for Josephine. The show opened in March 1924 at the Lyceum Theater in Rochester, New York, with a huge cast, lavish sets, and even three live horses in a simulated race. By the time it opened in New York City in September, the producers had changed the name to *The Chocolate Dandies* and Josephine was receiving $125 a week, a tremendous amount of money at that time. However, the show was not popular because it didn't have the unique black flavor of their previous play. White audiences expected stereotyped performances from blacks—plantation life, the Mississippi River, levees, bright-colored clothing, and turbans. Josephine's comic actions and silly faces didn't go with her costume—a clinging silk dress with a skirt slit up to the thighs, a sash, and a big bow.

The play got poor reviews, and its closing was inevitable. At the same time the show declined, Josephine received an invitation to appear at the Plantation Theater Restaurant in Harlem, a nightclub that was the birthplace of many stars' careers. The restaurant impressed Josephine with its elegant, brightly lit décor, starched tablecloths, and French-speaking waiters clad in tuxedos. Featured in the show that started after the theaters closed at midnight was singer Ethel Waters.

Ethel and Josephine roomed together, and the young woman strove to imitate the singer in every way. After she listened to Ethel singing her signature song "Dinah" several nights in a row, Josephine decided she wanted to become a singer as well as a dancer. She especially wanted to get out of the comic routine, so she started daily practices to change her high, thin, unclear singing voice to one more like Ethel's lower, husky tones. While she practiced, she memorized all of Ethel Waters's songs.

One day, Ethel developed laryngitis. Josephine went to see the director. She knocked on his door and told him, "I can sing all [of Ethel's] numbers." He nodded his willingness to listen. Josephine started singing but found "it was not easy to perform in an office in front of a man who stares at you as if you're some sort of bug." Nonetheless she convinced him she knew the songs and could perform them. He was impressed enough to allow her to go onstage in the star's stead.

That night the audience loved Josephine's act, and for the first time she received flowers from a male admirer. In her dressing room after the show, she discovered a vase of violets on the dressing table. One of the chorus girls told her that the flowers were a way of expressing appreciation for a wonderful

ETHEL WATERS

Born October 31, 1896, Ethel Waters rose from a poverty-stricken childhood to become one of the most popular blues and jazz singers of the 1920s. Her autobiography, *His Eye is on the Sparrow: An Autobiography,* details her early struggles before she achieved fame. With a rich voice that spanned two octaves and an innate talent for acting, she was able to scale the barriers that had previously kept black performers out of white theaters.

After touring in vaudeville shows as a singer and a dancer, Ethel moved to New York, where she sang "Dinah" at the Plantation Club with such success that Columbia Records signed her to a recording contract. A few years later, she acted in the first of many films and also became the first black performer to star in a sponsored coast-to-coast radio show. Her last years were spent touring with evangelist Billy Graham. She died from a heart condition in Chatsworth, California, on September 2, 1977, at the age of 80.

performance. Josephine wondered who had sent them, but she was unable to read the card because she was illiterate.

While they were on the road together, Clara Smith had tried to teach Josephine to improve her reading and writing. The young girl had learned only how to decipher the printed page. She could not read the handwritten note attached to the flowers. Some of the other chorus girls ridiculed her and called her stupid. Finally, the girl who had explained the significance of the flowers also read the card to her. It was signed by Henry, and the message said that he would meet her at the stage door after the show.

Later that night she was surprised to learn that Henry was a white young man with blue eyes and freckles. Because restaurants would not admit or serve black patrons, he took her to a bar in Greenwich Village, where artists of all kinds met. Throughout the evening, Henry praised Josephine. With his compliments ringing in her ears, she looked forward to singing the next night. However, Ethel had heard how much the audience liked her replacement, and she made a quick recovery. Josephine never sang again at the Plantation Club.

Though Josephine was disappointed, she accepted that Ethel Waters was the club's star and that she would get no more opportunities to sing there. But her admirer Henry attended all of Josephine's chorus line performances and continued to send her flowers.

Thinking Henry was interested in her romantically, Josephine asked to meet his parents. He agreed. On the night they had scheduled the introductions, Henry appeared with a parrot in a cage as a gift for Josephine. He was alone, though, because his parents did not want to meet her. Accepting that Henry would never marry her, Josephine began to think about what she wanted to do next.

In the meantime and unbeknownst to Josephine, Caroline Dudley Reagan, an American socialite in her thirties, planned to put together an all-black revue to perform in Paris, where segregation was not an issue. After seeing eight girls dance the Charleston at the Douglas, a small theater in a black neighborhood, Caroline felt as if a magnet were drawing her to produce a show with such astounding artists. Caroline, who was white, loved the fluid performances of the black dancers and wanted to take them to Paris to amaze audiences there. As the seed for her revue sprouted and grew, she decided that she wanted a fresh show, not a rendition of an old play like *The Chocolate Dandies*.

With her dream fully formed, Caroline Reagan sought financial backers for the new show. She convinced Rolf de Maré, a wealthy, Swedish-born patron of the arts, to finance getting the cast members. He agreed to pay for her to go to New York City and to hire up to 30 performers, whose transportation to France he would also support. Caroline arrived in New York City and began selecting the cast. At the Plantation Club, she invited Ethel Waters to become the show's female singer, but Ethel's demand for $500 per week exceeded the socialite's budget, and she withdrew the offer. Next, Caroline invited Josephine to be part of the revue's chorus line at $150 a week. Josephine was torn about what to do. She knew little about Paris and was unsure about traveling to a strange country across the ocean. Although she had heard that black people were accepted everywhere in France, she didn't know if that was true. Questions swirled through her mind. What if she didn't like it? How would she get home?

Caroline Reagan said: "Paris is the most beautiful city in the world. Think it over. I'll be back." By the time she returned, Josephine had heard about the attempt to get Ethel Waters for the show's singer and asked if she could have the part offered to the star. Not knowing the leggy dancer had developed a nice voice,

Caroline refused, telling her she needed her for a comic act. When she raised the offer to $250 a week, Josephine accepted.

Even after she accepted the job in Paris, Josephine changed her mind over and over. Years later, she reminisced, "I can only recall one single day of fear in my life. One day which lasted only one hour, maybe one minute . . . when fear grasped my brain, my heart, my guts with such force that everything seemed to come apart. It was September 15, 1925." Several friends encouraged Josephine to take the opportunity offered her. Despite her fears, she followed their advice; and when the *Berengaria* sailed out of the New York harbor on that September date, bound for France, 19-year-old Josephine was among the 25 cast members headed to Paris.

3

Joséphine Charms Paris

ON THEIR WAY TO FRANCE, JOSEPHINE and the rest of the black cast traveled in steerage, the worst accommodations on the *Berengaria*. The huge passenger ship was segregated because it was owned by an American company. The separation between blacks and whites became even more obvious when the captain feared a German mine, left over from World War I, was in the ship's path. The crew scrambled to get life belts on all passengers and to direct them to lifeboats. When they realized there were not enough boats, the crew informed the steerage passengers that they would leave the ship last. The cast, including Josephine, huddled in fear as sounds of pulleys moving lifeboats into place mingled with those of screaming children. Fortunately, there was no mine, and the ship continued on its course.

During the voyage Caroline Reagan organized a rehearsal for their French show. Josephine's role was to dance the Charleston, but she refused because she wanted to sing.

Caroline Reagan decided to let the stubborn young woman prove herself one way or the other. For hours Josephine practiced

THE CHARLESTON

The Charleston expressed the uninhibited enthusiasm and spirit of the young people of the 1920s. The dance became popular after being performed in a black Broadway musical called *Runnin' Wild*. The steps involved using both swaying arms and fast movement of the feet. Because it could be danced alone, in couples, or as part of a group, it appealed to almost all Americans, especially the rebellious young women of the 1920s known as flappers.

The origin of the dance can be traced to slaves who had brought their tribal customs and rhythmic music with them from Africa. Many of the enslaved people settled off the coast of Charleston, South Carolina, hence the dance's name. When African Americans finally achieved freedom from slavery, many moved north to Chicago and New York to get jobs. They took their syncopated music to those cities, where over time it evolved into ragtime, blues, and eventually jazz. No other dance form affected an entire generation the way the Charleston influenced the 1920s.

"Brown Eyes, Why Are You So Blue?" with the cast's musical director, Claude Hopkins. Their time together in rehearsal turned into a romantic interlude for the two, despite the fact that Claude's wife, Mabel, was also on the ship. The other chorus girls resented what Josephine was doing to the unsuspecting wife, and some of them even threatened to throw Josephine overboard.

On the night of the performance, when Josephine went onstage wearing a bright red dress that Caroline had bought her, she felt confident. She had no idea she would face a problem projecting her voice in the huge room with poor acoustics. As she sang, she couldn't seem to find the beat, and the orchestra completely drowned her out. Her voice cracked and she produced three off-key notes in quick succession. At the end of the song, the audience was silent. Josephine had flopped as a performer for the first time as. She vented her rage, embarrassment, and frustration at Caroline, claiming the socialite had set her up for failure. Josephine shouted at her, "You're fixin' t'kill me! I'm finished! I'm leavin' tomorrow." After reminding the angry young woman that they were in the middle of the Atlantic Ocean, Caroline recommended Josephine forget about singing and instead concentrate on perfecting her dancing and comic skills.

By the next morning Josephine had calmed down, but the experience had increased her sense of insecurity. She was subdued and scared when she knocked on Caroline's door to ask her, "Miz Dudley, why you choose me? Why you want me to come?"

The *Berengaria* docked in France on September 22, 1925, and the cast boarded a train for the 100-mile trip to Paris. At lunchtime, Josephine and the others were astounded to discover they could sit anywhere they wanted in the dining car. One of the cast members had previously been to Europe, and he assured them that it was always that way in France. To people accustomed to segregation in America, this was welcome news.

Josephine arrived in Paris wearing black-and-white checkered gardening overalls and a hat decorated with poppies, sunflowers, and daisies. Before many weeks passed, she would be among the most fashionably dressed in the city. As the cast members made their way to their hotel, the invigorating sights and sounds of Paris called to Josephine, but there was no time to explore. The cast had only 10 days to get their show ready for the opening performance.

Rehearsals began at the Théâtre des Champs-Elysées. For several days the cast practiced for long, exhausting hours, but the show did not come together. André Daven, the owner of the Théâtre des Champs-Elysées, became more and more worried as the days went by without improvement. The *Revue Nègre* was not what he had expected. There was too much tap dancing and too much noise. Maud de Forrest, the female lead singer, chose gospel songs and spirituals that did not fit the show. Daven also found the costumes ridiculous: high-button green shoes with red laces and hats decorated in fruit and flowers. He needed to redesign the entire show.

When Daven's attempts at improvement also failed, he sought help from Jacques Charles, a talented choreographer from the Moulin Rouge. Charles visited one of the rehearsals and saw possibilities in the *Revue* because it reminded him of shows he had seen in Harlem, New York. Charles, who could not speak English, used an interpreter to tell the cast: "You must let me shape this show or you'll have to go back on the boat. I want total obedience. This will be your only chance."

The sets were wrong too, but there was no time to change them so Charles focused on employing the natural rhythm of black entertainers to improve the show. He decided to feature Josephine dancing the Charleston. Even her uninhibited performance did not satisfy him, so he designed a new dance for her that he called the *danse sauvage*, or the "wild dance." The dance required Josephine to appear topless wearing only a satin bikini bottom covered in pink flamingo feathers. Around her ankles and wrists she would wear the same pink feathers. Her partner Joe Alex would wear a feather-covered loincloth along with the ankle and wrist decorations.

Josephine was initially shocked by the costume. She refused to appear in such a revealing outfit and she demanded to go back to the United States. In response, Jacques Charles told her she must perform one night before she could go home. Sobbing and sniffling, Josephine started to practice, and after that, she made no more requests to return to the United States. She later recalled the occasion: "The first time I had to appear in front of the Paris audience . . . I had to execute a dance rather . . . savage. I came on stage and . . . a frenzy took possession of me . . . seeing nothing, not even hearing the orchestra, I danced!"

During this time, Josephine also posed in the studio of Paul Colin, the artist commissioned to create posters for the *Revue Nègre*. He had seen Josephine dance in rehearsal and he believed she had a beautiful, flexible body that would be perfect for a poster.

The red-and-black posters of Josephine went up all over Paris. By the time *Revue Nègre* opened at midnight on October 2, 1925, excited patrons shoved aside the security guards to find seats. An air of anticipation permeated the theater as the performance began before a packed house. When the curtain opened, a musician playing a clarinet wandered across the stage. By the time the last notes faded, all of the cast, except Josephine, was onstage in front of a Mississippi River levee set.

With lips painted large in the style of blackface comedy and dressed in a torn shirt and ragged shorts, Josephine waddled from behind the curtain with her knees bent and spread apart. Extremely short hair plastered to her head emphasized her puffed-out cheeks and her crossed eyes. At first silence greeted her entrance on the stage. Gradually, the audience began to laugh, shout, tap their feet, and whistle. The sounds elated Josephine—the audience liked her. She left the stage with the noise echoing around her, only to be greeted by an irate director who said: "This isn't New York. In France they whistle when they *don't* like the act."

Josephine appeared in several more scenes before the wild *danse sauvage* began. She and the muscular Joe Alex entered

PAUL COLIN

Josephine Baker had known Paul Colin only a few hours before he was commissioned to design a poster for her role in the *Revue Nègre*. She was not accustomed to posing for portraits, especially not while nude, so when Colin indicated that she should remove her clothes, she refused. Undeterred, he sat down and began to sketch. Josephine could not sit still, so he drew her in motion. Gradually, as his calmness soothed her, she found herself in only her slip. A few more turns around the room, and she was nude. The resulting poster launched both of their careers.

Over Paul's career, he created 1,200 posters in both color and black and white, as well as 700 stage and film sets. In 1927 he produced a book filled with colorful lithographs called *Le Tumulte Noir*, or *The Black Tumult*, which became one of his most important works. During World War II, Paul created patriotic posters, but his most famous poster remained Josephine in her banana skirt. During the time Josephine and Paul worked together, the two established a close relationship, and it is widely believed that he was one of her many lovers. Paul Colin died on June 18, 1985, at the age of 92.

Josephine clowns with a clarinet, surrounded by French musicians, at age 19. She also played the saxophone, having learned to do so while traveling around the United States on the black vaudeville circuit. © *Bettmann/CORBIS*

the stage with him carrying her on his back, her legs wrapped around him. He gradually lowered her to the floor, where she began a frenetic shaking of her body. She moved her stomach, rotated her hips, and shook her rump. Never had Parisians seen such action on a stage. Audience reactions varied, with some people returning to see the show multiple times while others stomped out after the first few minutes, slamming the doors, and calling the show a disgrace.

When asked what she most remembered about her first performance in France, Josephine thought for a moment and replied, "Well, last night after the show was over, the theater was turned into a big restaurant. . . . And for the first time in my life, I was invited to sit at a table and eat with white people." That evening Josephine made an entrance into the supper party area on the arm of Paul Colin, who had chosen her ice-blue designer dress. After that night he continued as her escort and also gave her frequent fashion advice. Josephine became a celebrity in Paris and changed the spelling of her name to the French Joséphine. Everywhere she went, dressed in the height of fashion, reporters vied for interviews with her. Strangers stopped her on the street, seeking her autograph, but at that time she could barely write her name.

Joséphine decided to move from the hotel where the cast stayed to the smaller Hotel Fournet, where she could indulge her love of animals. Animals interested her, she said, because "they are as simple and as uncomplicated as babies." Joséphine purchased a parakeet, a parrot, two baby rabbits, and a pink pig she named Albert. None of the animals were house-trained and her apartment soon smelled like a barnyard. Visitors had difficulty finding a safe place to sit.

When Joséphine heard that snake was the newest fashion in Paris, she did not realize the term referred to snakeskin and not live reptiles. She purchased a real snake that she named Kiki and wore it as a necklace with her favorite black velvet dress. The snake stayed quiet because it was warm, but when she started to dance, he woke up and stuck out his tongue. Joséphine laughed. "No one wanted to dance with me anymore. Everybody was frightened. I had been noticed, that is what I wanted."

Press clippings about her piled up, some positive, some not so. Theater critic Henri Jeanson wrote, "As beautiful as the night. Joséphine Baker is the dream, the clown, the great sensation of the evening." Critic Robert de Flers, on the other hand, called her performance "lamentable transatlantic exhibitionism." Joséphine put the reviews into a notebook and studied them to begin learning French. At first, all she recognized was the name of the show, names of cast members, and her own name. She struggled to learn other words, not realizing that the journalistic style of writing was not typical of the kind of language used in ordinary conversation.

Paul Derval, director of the music hall known as Folies Bergère, saw one of Joséphine's performances and invited her to join his show the following season. Without telling Caroline Reagan, she signed a contract to appear in a show entitled *La Folie du Jour*. The *Revue* continued playing to sold-out crowds for 10 weeks, although initially they had been scheduled for only two. At the end of November, the show moved to a smaller theater, and the crowds became a trickle as Parisians sought the next sensation.

Caroline Reagan was not troubled by the smaller attendance because she had already planned for the cast to tour Europe. For the first time in her life, Joséphine did not want to leave a place. She confessed, "I had plotted to leave St. Louis. I had longed to leave New York; I yearned to remain in Paris. I loved everything about the city. It moved me as profoundly as a man moves a woman. Why must I take trains and boats that would carry me far from the friendly faces, the misty Seine."

Despite her reluctance, she left with the cast for Brussels in mid-December. No one in the show yet knew that she had signed a contract to perform at the Folies Bergère in mid-March. The *Revue Nègre* appeared for a week in Brussels at the Cirque Royal, where King Albert of Belgium watched one show. It was Joséphine's first time appearing before royalty. From Brussels, the cast moved to the Nelson-Theater in Berlin, where they opened on New Year's Eve. Joséphine loved Berlin, and the people of Berlin loved her. So many people wanted to see the show that there was only one ticket price, and people drew seat numbers from a jar as they entered the theater.

One night, the famous German theater and film director Max Reinhardt was in the audience. After the show, he invited Joséphine to become a student at his acting school. She turned him down because of her commitment to the Folies Bergère show, but she continued to think about the offer. At a party, a Frenchman told her he was looking forward to seeing her at the Folies. She said, "Don't count on it." The man, a friend of Paul Derval, told the Folies director what Joséphine had said. Derval was stunned. He had already invested money in multiple sets, a cast of 500 performers, 1,200 costumes, and had commissioned music for the $500,000 show in which Joséphine would appear.

He could not afford to lose his investment, so he sent an agent to Berlin to confront Joséphine. The enormous amount of money that had already been spent on the show did not impress her as much as learning that Irving Berlin would be one of the music's composers. She wanted to perform Berlin's tunes, so she agreed to honor the contract. But remembering her childhood poverty and thus never missing an opportunity to make money, Joséphine told the agent, "If you want me to leave Berlin, it will cost an extra 400 francs ($100 in US dollars) a show." Her full salary would be more than $5,000 a month. Derval had no choice but to agree. All that remained for Joséphine to do was to tell Caroline Reagan she was leaving the show.

Caroline was furious. Even in later years, Joséphine showed no sympathy for the situation in which she had left Caroline. Instead, she saw herself as the aggrieved one. "I felt like kicking everyone in sight. Why couldn't people leave me alone?" With her star gone, the producer had to cancel the rest of the tour. After paying the cast members and providing passage for those who wanted to return to the United States, Reagan found herself $10,000 in debt. She started to sue Joséphine for that amount, but in the end she couldn't bring herself to do it.

Years later Joséphine told a reporter that she returned to Paris with trepidation. "I never recognized my having taken Paris by storm. I have never recognized, felt, nor understood that I was successful." Full of such misgivings, she returned to the city of her earlier triumphs to begin rehearsals for *La Folie du Jour*.

4

La Folie du Jour

THE YEAR 1926 WAS A PERFECT TIME for Joséphine to perform at the Folies Bergère music hall. Europe was recovering from the horrors of World War I, and people wanted more and more entertainment. In the evenings, the new three-story theater that housed the Folies held packed audiences. During the day, activity flourished. Craftsmen of all kinds worked in the building's basement. From makeup artists and costume designers to carpenters and electricians, everyone concentrated on producing a vibrant show. Seamstresses added miles of sequins to the multiple costumes made from over 30 miles of fabric that could stretch from New York to Boston. In the performance area, musicians practiced in the orchestra pit while builders constructed collapsible stairs and three-dimensional sets onstage.

The performances at the Folies included a wide variety of songs, sketches, acrobats, jugglers, and mimes. Joséphine, the star of the show, along with the rest of the huge cast, rehearsed around the clock for six weeks, preparing for the opening night of *La Folie du Jour*. As always, a superstitious Derval had selected

THE FOLIES BERGÈRE

The first music hall in Paris, the Folies Bergère, opened on May 2, 1869. Fashioned after music halls in London, it drew aristocrats and royal families from all over Europe. While seated at tables, patrons observed a mix of operettas, comic opera, popular songs, and gymnastics. However, such shows did not impress Parisians. Not until 1886, when new management featured chorus girls in scanty, revealing costumes—and later, bare-breasted women—did it become the city's hot spot.

The word *folies* is a synonym for theaters. At the time, tradition dictated that Paris theaters take their name from their location. Bergère was a street near the theater, so the structure became the Folies Bergère. Around the time of World War I, a new owner, Paul Derval, took over. His shows featured fancy costumes and fabulous sets along with nude or practically nude dancing women. The shows also included vaudeville, operettas, ballet, acrobats, jugglers, tightrope walkers, and magicians. Many 20th-century stars got their start at the Folies.

a title with exactly 13 letters because the one time he veered from the pattern, the show flopped. In the entrance to the theater hung huge animated color posters of Joséphine, and for the first time her name appeared in lights on the marquee.

In rehearsals, Joséphine's high energy level inspired the workers and the other actors to push themselves to their limits. However, her wild and unpredictable mood swings puzzled and

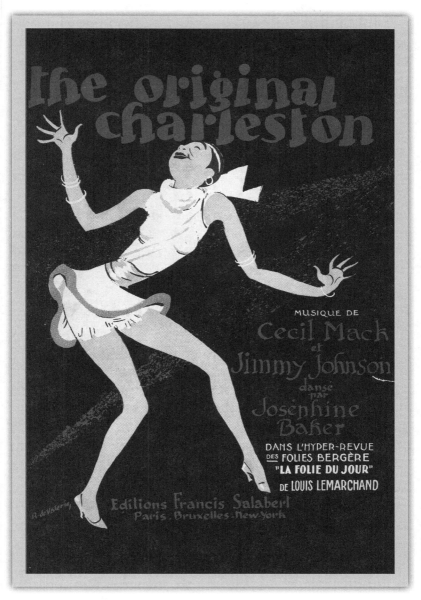

Poster from *La Folie du Jour* staged in Paris in 1926.
© *Leonard de Selva/Corbis*

irritated the cast and crew. She could go from uncontrollable sobbing to unrestrained enthusiasm and back again in a matter of minutes.

Adding to the emotional stress of working with Joséphine was her constant tardiness. Often the stage manager found himself standing on a corner outside the theater searching for Joséphine's car mere minutes before the curtain rose. The orchestra prepared extra songs just in case Joséphine was late, and sometimes the director changed the order of the acts while they awaited Joséphine's arrival. Derval recalled one instance when she burst in after slamming the stage door: "A hat went flying, a fur coat was flung to the floor. Leaving a trail of clothes, shoes, and underwear, Joséphine Baker tore past me *en route* to her dressing room."

Once she arrived at the dressing room, there was no guarantee of better behavior. One evening when she was due onstage, the stage manager came to get her. When she did not answer his knocks on her door, he kicked the door open only to find a naked Joséphine sitting on the floor and eating lobster with her fingers. She exasperated the seamstresses, often walking out as they knelt to pin in a hem. "I don't have the calling to be a pincushion," she told them.

Joséphine further irritated Derval with the menagerie of animals she kept at the theater. She considered every kind of animal her friend and claimed her pets would never let her down as so many people had. "I tell them everything, my joys, my hurts," said Joséphine, who had rabbits nesting in the wardrobes, white mice in the drawers, and cats, dogs, and birds everywhere. A baby tiger and a boa constrictor completed the odd mixture.

On the stage for *La Folie du Jour*, Joséphine first appeared in a jungle scene. Dressed only in a skirt of 16 rubber bananas placed vertically and attached to a cloth girdle, she entered the stage walking backward on her hands and bare feet with her legs and arms held stiff. Then she stretched her arms back like the wings of a giant bird and moved along a fallen tree trunk. A young white explorer slept on the riverbank. In the background drums beat a wild rhythm. Joséphine began to dance. With every movement of her flexible body, the bananas swayed up and down, often looking as if, in the frenzy, they would fly away. The audience screamed, stomped, and catcalled. For the rest of her life, Joséphine was largely remembered for her dance in the banana skirt.

To emphasize his star's energetic personality, Derval needed a spectacular way to bring her onstage at the end of the show. He decided to place her in a huge egg-shaped iron cage that was painted gold and entwined with roses. Steel cables held the egg suspended above the stage until it descended from the rafters and reached the stage floor. A gate opened to reveal a mirror on which Joséphine lay. She was nude except for a skirt of silk fringes and a feather necklace. Rising slowly and seductively, she began to dance on the mirror. Lights reflected from the mirror and threw shadow images all over the theater. When the dance concluded, the egg closed and the cables started to pull it back up. Then one night, something went awry. One of the cables jammed and caused the cage to tilt. Trapped on the slippery mirror, Joséphine began to slide out of the dangling cage, 45 feet above the orchestra. Somehow, she grabbed the edge of the mirror and managed to hold on until stagehands rescued her.

As a whole the show received criticism for being too extravagant, but Joséphine received only accolades. Her new, more glamorous image brought praise, and poet e.e. cummings, writing for *Vanity Fair*, marveled at the change in her persona from her role in *The Chocolate Dandies*, when she appeared as a "tall, vital, incomparably fluid nightmare which crossed its eyes and warped its limbs in a purely unearthly manner" to become the most beautiful star on the Parisian stage.

By autumn, Joséphine's name was everywhere in Paris as she endorsed cocktails, swimsuits, perfumes, creams, and pomades to slick down hair and achieve her plastered look. The hair product, called Bakerfix, was a best seller for the next 30 years and brought her more cash than anything but her stage appearances. Dolls clad in banana skirts sold by the thousands.

Money rolled in, and Joséphine enjoyed only the best, most expensive French products—chocolates made by the Marquise de Sévigné and clothing made by her own dressmaker, Maison Jane. Her luxury car was a Delage and her radio a Vitus. Her Charleston dancing inspired the fashion world, and skirts became shorter to accommodate the dance's movements.

Her lateness aside, Joséphine was popular with the show's cast, and on June 3, 1926, they threw a 20th birthday party for her. They showered her with gifts—perfume, scarves, bracelets, and a puppy. Despite this show of friendship, Joséphine was lonely and began to party away most nights. "After the show at the Folies, I began appearing at various cabarets, where I danced the Charleston until the wee hours. . . . At dawn I would head home." Between the Folies and her moonlighting, she worked 18-hour days.

One of her favorite cabarets was owned by a short black woman named Ada Smith, who had nicknamed herself "Bricktop" because of the red dye in her hair. Pale-skinned and slightly plump, she had a nice voice and a warm personality that attracted crowds to her place. Joséphine struck up a friendship with Bricktop, who became both a mentor and a lover to the younger woman. Their relationship lasted for the rest of their lives.

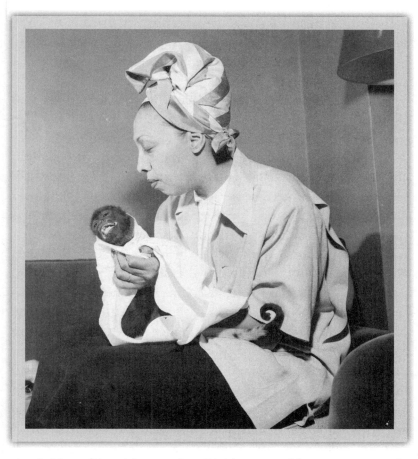

Joséphine with spider monkey Binki, rescued from a pet store in Rio de Janeiro. © *Bettmann/CORBIS*

Then Joséphine met Marcel Ballot, the wealthy owner of a large automobile company. They began an affair, and he lavished presents upon her, including the construction of a marble swimming pool in the middle of her apartment. Whenever he came to visit, he always brought an animal surprise: white mice, parrots, and a miniature monkey.

Joséphine believed such generosity was a prelude to commitment. She decided she wanted to have a baby with him and broached the subject of marriage, conveniently forgetting she was still wed to Willie Baker.

Marcel squelched the idea. In blunt words, he told her that she was not his social equal and she was black—not marriage material for him. Devastated by his words, Joséphine lost her pep and energy. She became ill, and the doctor diagnosed bronchial pneumonia. In those days before the availability of penicillin, this was a serious disease. Joséphine developed a high fever and was confined to bed for three weeks. She gradually recovered and regained her strength. In October, she made her first record with Odeon Records, which included the song "Bye, Bye, Blackbird."

Despite her recent illness, Joséphine spent her evenings partying in Montmartre, an area in Paris that nurtured most of the great artists and writers living in France at that time. It was in Montmartre that she met a man who had a great influence on her future. Giuseppe "Pepito" Abatino was a 37-year-old Italian bricklayer who had created a fake family history for himself and changed his name to Count Abatino. The fake royal title appealed to the ladies, with whom he was quite popular.

Of middle height with dark hair, a dark mustache, and dark eyes, Pepito wore a monocle and carried a walking cane, adding to his aura of sophistication. After meeting Joséphine, he pursued her with love notes during the day and escorted her to clubs and cabarets in the evenings. He flattered her and treated her like a lady—opening doors and pulling out chairs. Joséphine was charmed. He helped hold at bay her fear that she would disappear from the stage and be forgotten. Her mentor Bricktop did not like Pepito and advised Joséphine not to have a relationship with him.

MONTMARTRE

North of Paris on a 427-foot-high hill is Montmartre, which was once a rural village of vineyards and windmills. Montmartre means "mount of martyrs" and refers to the beheading of St. Denis, the first Paris bishop, in 250 AD. Initial settlers on Montmartre were refugees from Paris when Emperor Napoleon III gave much of the best land in the city to his wealthy friends.

Montmartre became a popular drinking area which began to attract artists, performers, and entertainment sites. Even as these groups took over Montmartre, it retained some of its distinct characteristics: old buildings; steep, narrow streets; and rustic windmills, some of which still operate today. Gradually, it became a working-class neighborhood, and by the time of the Paris World's Fair in 1900, it had developed into an entertainment district with cabarets, dance halls, music halls, theaters, and circuses. Today Montmartre is a popular tourist destination.

As usual, the headstrong Joséphine ignored any advice, and Pepito became her manager and her lover. He decided she should not waste her time, energy, and money on frequenting other people's clubs. He suggested she open her own establishment and he found a wealthy doctor to finance Chez Joséphine, which opened on December 14, 1926, in Pigalle, a tourist district in Paris. Customers flocked to the small club and paid exorbitant

Joséphine Baker with Pepito (Count Abatino) after he became her manager and lover. © *Bettmann/CORBIS*

prices for the food just for a chance to be close to Joséphine and perhaps talk to her.

Her new manager never lost an opportunity to promote her, and he found a man to help Joséphine write her memoirs. Marcel Sauvage became the collaborator of her first book, *Les Mémoires de Joséphine Baker*, or *The Memoirs of Joséphine Baker*, while Paul Colin, the artist who created her first poster for the *Revue Nègre*, designed the book cover. Although she was only 21 years old, the memoirs portrayed her personality and contained opinions on a wide variety of subjects from her favorite meals to why she liked animals better than people. Like a child, she recalled gifts received: "I got sparkling rings as big as eggs, 150-year-old earrings that once belonged to a duchess, pearls like buck teeth, flower baskets from Italy . . . lots of stuffed animals . . . a pair of gold shoes, four fur coats, and bracelets with red stones for my arms and legs." She also included recipes for meals that she had enjoyed as a child, such as corned beef hash and hotcakes. Some of her memories were inaccurate, such as her assertion that her parents were married (they were not). Other recollections were fanciful. In her dreams, kings walked with pointed shoes "and the queens were blond . . . sometimes I cried because I too would have liked to be a queen."

Perhaps the most startling revelation of the memoir was her attitude about performing onstage. She said, "I am tired of this artificial life, weary of being spurred on by the footlights. The work of a star disgusts me now. Everything she must do, everything she must put up with at every moment, that star, disgusts me." In commenting on the future, she predicted,

> I will marry an average man. I will have children, plenty of pets. This is what I love. I want to live in peace surrounded by children and pets. But if one day one of my children wants to go into the music hall, I will strangle him with my own two hands, that I swear to you.

This reflected the conflict that Joséphine dealt with all her life. She longed for a happy home life but could not resist the footlights' pull.

While she and Sauvage worked on her memoirs, Joséphine also starred in *Un Vent de Folie*, or *A Wind of Madness*, a second Folie production that Paul Derval produced with her as the star. The mixed audience reactions to *Un Vent de Folie* indicated that Joséphine's popularity was slipping because people were tired of seeing the same type of performances. She received attention of a different sort in the spring of 1927, when she passed her driving test. The driving school where she had trained took out a full-page ad in the newspaper announcing that Joséphine had been their student.

In the evenings, after the *Folie* show, she went to Chez Joséphine, where she often sang—a prelude to her later career as a singer. Listening to her each night were her goat Toutoute and her pig Albert, who lived at the club. Of all the people who regularly came to her club, a famous writer named Sidonie-Gabrielle Colette was her favorite. Short and plump with short, frizzy hair and lips painted in a hard, thin line, Colette had no physical beauty to attract Joséphine to her, but earning the attention of the most famous female French writer of her time flattered Joséphine. She soon discovered she had much in common with the 52-year-old Colette, despite their age difference. Both had started in music halls, and both enjoyed shocking audiences, whether appearing nude or in lesbian scenes. Colette later dedicated a book to Joséphine, although it is not likely that Joséphine could have read much of it. The two became close friends and lovers in a relationship that lasted many years.

As Paris welcomed an influx of Americans, racial attitudes changed. One night while Joséphine sang, an American man shouted out that back in his country, she would be in the kitchen, not performing. That prejudice was infiltrating France became even more apparent when a hotel manager refused to rent Joséphine a suite because he feared her presence in the hotel would offend his American guests. Despite these unsettling incidents, Joséphine continued to work on new projects. She began a film called *La Siréne Des Tropiques*, or *The Siren of the Tropics*, but Joséphine did not enjoy the restrictions of filming as opposed to performing onstage. She resented having to confine her actions to a limited space and having to accommodate camera angles and lighting.

While she struggled with these demands, she received sad news about her favorite little sister: Willie Mae had become pregnant at 17 years old, and she died while trying to terminate the pregnancy. The frustration of making the movie and the grief over her sister caused Joséphine to become even more difficult to work with. Although rehearsals started on the set at nine in the morning, she'd arrive at five in the afternoon, storm into her dressing room, slam the door, and begin smashing makeup bottles against the wall. When someone once dared to ask what the matter was, she replied that her dog was sick.

Needing a new way to regain attention for Joséphine, she and Pepito announced that they had married at the American embassy on her 21st birthday. The marriage was as phony as Pepito's title of Count. But Derval capitalized on the sham marriage by placing posters all over town claiming Joséphine was now a countess. She played her part well, acting the bubbly, giddy bride at a press conference: "I'm just as happy as I can be. I didn't have any idea that getting married was exciting. I feel like I'm sitting on pins and needles. I am so thrilled." To add to her remarks, she flashed a 16-carat diamond wedding ring that she claimed she could not wear often because of its weight. She also announced that the count had given her all the jewelry and heirlooms belonging to his royal family.

After finding no record of the marriage, French reporters doubted the story, but American papers picked it up with headlines proclaiming that a young black woman from St. Louis had become a countess. The June 22, 1927, issue of the *Milwaukee Journal* headlined: JOSEPHINE BAKER, BLACK DANCER, WEDS A REAL COUNT. They quoted Joséphine as saying: "He sure is a count. I looked him up in Rome. He's got a great big family there with lots of coats of arms and everything." This was good news for black Americans who still faced racial prejudice in the

United States. Probably the most surprised person was Willie Baker, who read the story in the *Chicago Defender*. Despite what he may have thought, he did not challenge Joséphine's apparent bigamy. Later some diligent reporters, having determined that there was no marriage record and that the count title was fake, learned that the whole episode was a publicity stunt. Joséphine dropped the countess title. By the time the sham was discovered, she had tired of what she was doing. Her contract with Derval for the Folies performances was coming to an end. Pepito decided to focus on making her as famous as possible, and he arranged a long tour to 25 countries in Europe and South America.

Before starting the tour, Joséphine gave a farewell show in Paris to demonstrate her development as a performer. In the first act, dressed in the torn shorts and ragged shirt of previous performances, she danced the Charleston. The audience seemed indifferent—they had seen it before. In the second act, however, she returned to the stage wearing a long, well-cut, red dress, and on her head she wore a fitted cloche studded with rhinestones. She sang in French for the first time and made a brief farewell speech, also in that language. She should have quit with the audience cheering her. Instead she began to thank all the people who had helped her. The long list was printed in the program, so it was not necessary for her to call them to the stage. At the intermission she further bored the audience by auctioning off five signed programs. By the time she got to the third one, catcalls and boos filled the theater.

Pepito hoped that Joséphine's absence would return her to the hearts of the French people. While they toured, he planned to transform her into a proper lady by hiring language tutors, polishing her table manners, and teaching her the art of conversation. The couple departed France in January 1928, headed for their first stop in Vienna, Austria. Until their arrival in the city, they did not realize it was embroiled in political turmoil. A socialist government ruled the country, and 100,000 workers walked the streets looking for employment. Most of these workers were ready to unite with Germany because Austrians had begun to believe the ideas found in Adolf Hitler's autobiographical manifesto, *Mein Kampf,* or *My Struggle,* in which he used insulting terms for black people, whom he considered inferior to whites. Before Joséphine ever arrived in Vienna, posters and flyers called her the "black devil," and a petition circulated to prevent her performance.

Another group did not want Joséphine to perform in their city on moral grounds. Priests warned the large Catholic population to stay off the streets when she came so that they would not come into contact with her. To help people avoid her, St. Paul's rang its church bells in warning as soon as her train arrived in the city. On the way to her hotel in a horse-drawn carriage, Joséphine was frightened to see protestors lining the streets. They brought back memories of her childhood and the East St. Louis riots when she was 11.

The city council refused to let Joséphine perform at the Ronacher Theater as previously scheduled, so Pepito booked her at another, smaller theater, the Johann Strauss. Since it was not available until four weeks later, they used the extra time to explore Vienna and for Joséphine to learn how to ski at a nearby alpine resort.

Despite the protests, many Viennese welcomed her on opening night. The theater was filled and continued to be so for the next three weeks. Instead of appearing onstage in the banana skirt expected by the audience, Joséphine wore a long cream dress buttoned up to the neck and sang a simple spiritual, "Pretty Little Baby," in English. The audience applauded and rose to their feet. After she opened the show with such a demure performance, they accepted the other acts in which she danced more provocatively.

The next stop was the jazz-loving city of Prague, where a huge crowd welcomed Joséphine at the train station. As she tried to move from the train to her limousine, her fans stampeded to see her. She jumped on top of the car to avoid being crushed. The incident frightened her, but she stayed on the car's roof as she rode through the town, waving to the crowds. At the theater, when she concluded her last act, the audience threw rabbit feet on the stage. It was well known that Joséphine always carried a rabbit foot with her for good luck, and her audience wanted to increase her luck with their gifts.

Joséphine loved Budapest, where again, such large crowds welcomed her that she hid in a hay wagon to get away. However, not everyone wanted her to perform in their city, which at that time battled widespread poverty. On opening night, angry militant students threw ammonia bombs on the stage when she appeared at the Royal Orpheum Theater. They resented a foreigner making so much money when there were so many poor people in their country. The incident alarmed Joséphine, but she did not stop her performance. The following day, Pepito added to the publicity surrounding the agitators' actions by having Joséphine ride through downtown Budapest in a small buggy pulled by an ostrich. Thankfully Joséphine did not encounter any more explosive receptions after leaving Budapest. In Stockholm, the entire royal family, headed by the Crown Prince of Sweden, came to see her show. When asked what the Crown Prince looked like, Joséphine said, "I couldn't tell you. When I dance, I dance. I don't look at anyone, not even a king."

As they moved on, a tragedy occurred in Zagreb, Croatia. Alexius Groth, a 21-year-old draftsman, first saw Joséphine in

Budapest and was so fascinated by her that he followed her tour. He flooded her with flowers and love notes, but she ignored him. One night as she left a nightclub, the young man walked right up to her and pulled out a knife. Instead of using it on Joséphine, Alexius stabbed himself and fell at her feet. The *New York Times* reported: "He wounded himself severely but may recover." Once again Joséphine was thoroughly frightened by her fans' reaction to her, but she continued to perform nonetheless.

The tour's last stop in Europe was Amsterdam, where enthusiastic crowds jammed the streets for two hours. Joséphine danced the Charleston in Dutch clogs, and her performance was so successful that the show was booked for twice as long as originally planned.

Joséphine and Pepito went back to Paris in the summer of 1929. They immediately visited the newspaper offices to make sure everyone knew she had returned and to show them how well she could speak French. Even though Joséphine had to complete her tour, she told the newsmen, "I don't want to live without Paris. It's my country. The Charleston, the bananas—finished. Understand? I have to be worthy of Paris. I want to become an artist."

5

Two Loves

IN THE SAME YEAR THAT THE Great Depression began in America, Joséphine bought a mansion in Le Vésinet, a suburb about 15 miles from the heart of Paris. Called Le Beau Chêne, or The Beautiful Oak, the 30-room, red-and-gray, brick house sat on extensive grounds covered with stately oaks. High metal gates guarded the entrance to a long white gravel driveway leading to the house that looked like a castle, with its turrets and dormer windows. The spacious grounds also included a formal garden, a terrace, a greenhouse, several lily ponds filled with goldfish, and enough land for Joséphine's menagerie of animals: dogs, cats, monkeys, parrots, parakeets, cockatiels, rabbits, piglets, turtles, ducks, chickens, geese, pigeons, pheasants, and turkeys.

To Joséphine, Le Beau Chêne was a dream come true. Her friend Bricktop said, "Joséphine had to have been here before as a queen or something. She traipsed around her château just like she always lived this way. . . I think she thought she was Napoleon's Josephine."

To get rid of the mansion's interior gloominess, Joséphine remodeled and decorated each room in a unique design, from the style of Louis XVI to East Indian decor. In her own suite, she placed a silver-plated bathtub. For furnishings, she purchased antiques, such as a 15th-century suit of armor for the entrance hall. She hired three gardeners and gave them their first assignment: across the terrace, spell out JOSÉPHINE BAKER, using yellow- and red-leafed coleus plants.

Before she completed the plans for the new home, Joséphine and Pepito sailed for South America to finish her world tour. This voyage, in which she stayed in a first-class cabin, differed greatly from the one four years earlier, when she traveled from the United States to France in steerage on the *Berengaria*. Joséphine expected to find racial tolerance in South America, but when she and Pepito docked in Buenos Aires, Argentina, in the summer of 1929, she was shocked to discover that she was a source of controversy. Demonstrators protesting her presence mingled in the streets with people who were anti-government. Protestors for one cause or another seemed to be everywhere.

On opening night, agitators from both groups filled the theater. They hurled abusive language at each other and threw firecrackers, many of which landed on the stage. Joséphine huddled in fear behind the stage curtains. The orchestra kept on playing until the disruption ceased. Then Joséphine danced before a full house of 2,500 people. After that, the theater sold out for every night of her performances, leading her to feel that much of the protest concerned her race, not her dancing. The trip marked a turning point for her. For the first time, she recognized that racial prejudice was not limited to the United States. That realization affected the rest of her life. She became determined to prove that all people, regardless of race, should be treated the same because they were all part of one family. Skin color should not matter.

From Buenos Aires, Joséphine and Pepito traveled by train through the Andes Mountains to Chile, where 20,000 people waited. She loved looking at the natural scenery as they moved on to Brazil and Uruguay. While she was in South America, Joséphine's movie debut, *La Sirène des Tropiques* opened at the Lafayette Theater in Harlem, New York, on September 20, 1929. New York City's mayor, James J. Walker, attended the performance; it was the first time a New York mayor had gone to a Harlem theater. But the film did not receive good reviews. One columnist wrote: "The closest I can come to telling what it is like is to say that five minutes of her acting in an American studio would cause the director to hit her in the head with the camera." Black audiences also criticized Joséphine for abandoning her American roots and her native language in the French film. However, since she wasn't in New York, she wasn't bothered by any of it.

Joséphine finished her performances in South America and left Rio de Janeiro on the SS *Lutetia* just before Christmas of 1929. While they toured the world, Pepito had hired French, Spanish, and German tutors to improve Joséphine's language skills. He helped her develop her own fashion style and gave her lessons in table manners. She left Paris a clown; she returned a lady. The changes both pleased and worried her. She wondered about the reception of the "new" Joséphine in Paris. Would Parisians like her as a polished performer?

But it wasn't Joséphine's personal changes that presented challenges when they returned. They found the theaters in crisis because the new talking movies had captivated audiences. Instead of seeking immediate stage performances for her, Pepito decided to reintroduce Joséphine to Paris through a variety of social events. His work paid off, and he got her a contract to star in a revue at the Casino de Paris, the most respectable of the city's music halls in the 1930s. Henri Varna ran the club, which emphasized singing and dancing more than nudity.

For many years, a 54-year-old woman who went by the stage name Mistinguett had reigned over the Casino as its chief performer, but Varna believed a staged rivalry between the two women would attract more patrons.

MISTINGUETT, QUEEN OF THE MUSIC HALL

From childhood, Jeanne Marie Bourgeois wanted to perform in the French music halls. Although she did not have a great voice, could not dance well, and was not a physical beauty, she had gorgeous legs which were at one time insured for 500,000 francs (in today's value, $560,000). More important, she possessed a forceful personality that radiated from the stage. When she was 12 years old, she rode the trains into Paris every day to be around singers, dancers, and actors. To get money for the trips, she sold flowers at the entrance to the Casino de Paris.

After she appeared in a few shows, she adopted the nickname Mistinguett. A songwriting friend had made up the name Miss Tinguette. Jeanne Marie liked it and, after dropping a couple of letters, she came up with her stage name: Mistinguett. In her performances, she introduced the practice of a show's star making her entrance from the top of a staircase. Mistinguett performed in both the United States and England but was never as popular in those countries as she was in France.

Varna hired Joséphine to star in the 1930–31 show called *Paris qui Remue*, or *Swinging Paris*, and he planned to alternate the years in which Mistinguett and Joséphine starred. Mistinguett objected strongly to the shared show. She also complained about the director's purchase of a cheetah for her rival's menagerie. The cheetah, named Chiquita, went everywhere with Joséphine on a leash attached to a diamond collar valued at $20,000. Later, Joséphine bought Chiquita a collar to match each of her outfits, making the performer and her big cat prime advertisements for the show.

Before rehearsals began, Mistinguett enlisted the aid of Earl Leslie, the show's choreographer and her boyfriend, to make practices difficult for the young performer. Traditionally, Mistinguett entered the stage by descending a golden staircase. She did not want Joséphine to copy her, so Earl complained to Varna. He said Joséphine did not have the poise to make such a dramatic entrance. To counter the objection, Varna worked with Joséphine to improve her posture. Balancing first two books, and eventually six, on her head, she descended the stairs time and time again until she could do it with confidence.

Mistinguett made one more attempt to get rid of the woman challenging her place at the Casino by starting a fight with Joséphine in public. Both women attended a movie premiere, and when the older star saw Joséphine in the theater's lobby, she called out to her using a racial epithet. Joséphine forgot all the "ladylike" training Pepito had provided her. She grabbed Mistinguett's arm and dug her fingernails into the woman's flesh. At the same time she spit in her adversary's face. Mistinguett spat back before others separated them.

Although the show was scheduled to open on September 26, 1930, a string of misfortunes made that date questionable. A chorus girl sprained her ankle, a costume in the "Electricity" sketch short-circuited, and the wind machine stopped working.

Joséphine loved animals as well as the impression she created strolling through the streets of Paris with one of her big cats. For performers to have exotic pets was considered chic.
© *Hulton-Deutsch Collection/CORBIS*

All of the tension upset Chiquita, who chewed a hole in the leg of one of the dancer's pants. Joséphine was glad she had all those rabbit feet in the dressing room. Her luck held and on opening night Joséphine appeared at the top of the staircase as a white-plumed forest bird wrapped in huge swan feathers. With charm and grace, she descended the steps while 11 projectors bathed her in flickering lights. She reached the bottom and winked at the audience as if mocking what she had just done.

Each sketch in *Paris qui Remue* represented a different French colony, and Joséphine appeared in all of them. In one scene, she sang a song written especially for her—"J'ai Deux Amours," or "I Have Two Loves," referring to her own country and Paris, as well as perhaps sending a coded message of her bisexuality. She and the audiences both loved the song, and she sang it at every performance for the rest of her life.

In one emotional scene that protested cruelty to animals, Joséphine again appeared with wings attached to her body. This time they were made of a delicate transparent fabric and resembled those of a dragonfly. She walked down a steel ramp to the stage that had been transformed into a forest, where fierce hunters appeared and pretended to attack her. She begged them to stop and even escaped for a moment. They circled around her, tore her wings from her body, and left her huddled in despair on the stage floor. Many in the audience were moved to tears by Joséphine's performance. A review the next day said: "The beautiful savage has learned to discipline her instincts . . . Her singing, like a wounded bird, transported the crowd." *Paris qui Remue* was so popular that it ran for 481 performances during the 1931 season. To Mistinguett's dismay, her nemesis's shows drew larger crowds than her own.

One night, Joséphine was surprised by a visit from Noble Sissle, the playwright who had featured her in *Shuffle Along* and

The Chocolate Dandies in the United States. He invited her to return to America and star in the new version of *Shuffle Along* that he was producing. The invitation was tempting, and the idea of being a star in her own country appealed to Joséphine. However, she didn't know how her home country would receive her. Furthermore, Joséphine believed she could do more to advance race relations by performing with interracial casts in Paris than with all-black casts in the United States. Ultimately she declined Sissle's offer and stayed in Paris.

In 1931, the Paris Colonial Exposition took place to celebrate France's colonial empire. Just before the exposition opened, officials invited Joséphine to be "Queen of the Colonies." Since most of France's territories were in Africa, choosing an African American star seemed appropriate for the show's theme. Joséphine viewed the invitation as an indication of her acceptance by the general population. However, many of the French still regarded her as a foreigner, even though she claimed Paris as one of her two loves. To her dismay, the appointment caused an uproar. Crowds protested that she was not a French woman. Others claimed she did not speak either French or any of the colonies' dialects with native fluency. The biggest insult, as far as Joséphine was concerned, was objectors' arguing she was too old. At the time, some African women were wed at 12 or 13 years of age. By the time they reached Joséphine's age of 25, they were often grandmothers. Officials bowed to public pressure and withdrew the offer.

While she enjoyed great success at the Casino, Joséphine began to separate her life into two parts: the popular, glamorous performer and the quiet homebody. For her role as a star at the Casino de Paris, Joséphine wore exciting, expensive dresses, drove a car, and signed autographs. At home at Le Beau-Chêne, she wore simple skirts and blouses. Joséphine raised orchids in

1931 PARIS COLONIAL EXPOSITION

The Paris Colonial Exposition opened on May 6, 1931, in a huge park outside eastern Paris. The event offered the French government an opportunity to convince its citizens of the value of having colonies of native peoples that the French government controlled in places such as Guinea, Morocco, Martinique, and Cambodia. For the mammoth display, the government brought native people from its various colonies to Paris, where they were placed in housing similar in design but much larger in scope than what they had in their home countries. One of the most impressive buildings was the massive reproduction of a Cambodian temple, Angkor Wat.

While over 33 million visitors paraded past the people in their native costumes, the colonists practiced their crafts and demonstrated their music and dance. The French government displayed the colonies as part of greater France and showed resources supposedly available to the French people. However, the displays were a sham that did not truly represent life in the colonies. People did not regularly wear native costumes, and the displays depicted a misleading sampling of their lives. In reality, colonial resources added to the government's power and wealth rather than to that of its citizens. However, for the most part, French citizens accepted the government's premise that the diverse cultures and huge resources of the colonies were good for France.

the greenhouse, visited her menagerie of animals, and planted onions, potatoes, cabbage, and black-eyed peas in her vegetable garden.

Unfortunately, the unpredictable behavior of her professional life carried over to her home life. According to Hélene Guignery, wife of the electrician who rewired Le Beau-Chêne, "She could be very bossy with her employees, even cruel sometimes, especially if she thought they were fooling around, not doing their jobs." She might be playing with the cats or working in the garden when a single word or gesture by an employee could bring on a temper tantrum. Her rapid mood changes might come once a day, twice a day, or only once a week. Sometimes a crisis lasted a whole week.

Part of her stress came from Pepito's constant pushing her to keep moving upward in the performance world. The more she relaxed in their country home, the more she rebelled against him. She showed her displeasure by shopping for clothes—buying an outrageous number of pieces she did not need. Joséphine associated clothes with her beloved grandmother who had given them to her for dress-up and for performances in her basement. Her grandmother always told her granddaughter how pretty she looked, and Joséphine related clothes to love, something for which she still yearned.

She also longed to have a child, but in the meantime, she visited the children at St. Charles Orphanage in her neighborhood. She donated clothes, furs, jewelry, and knickknacks to raise money for the orphans to visit the ocean. She became godmother to all 50 children at the institution. She built a playground with swings and slides on the grounds of her own home and invited the orphans to play there and enjoy the many animals she kept. At Christmas Joséphine gave a party that included a gift for each child. She loved the children and associated that

feeling with her love for her animals—all of them being innocent and pure. A companion who helped her deliver the gifts
said, "The sight of Josephine picking up the little ones, stroking
their heads, made tears come to my eyes. This was not done for
effect, or for an audience."

The show at the Casino de Paris ended in the fall of 1931.
Since it was Mistinguett's turn to star in the next revue, Joséphine went on another tour, this time with her own band of jazz
musicians that she called the Sixteen Baker Boys. Everywhere
they went, they were met with enthusiasm and praise. While
Joséphine was touring, she received news that her cheetah Chiquita had escaped the grounds of Le Beau-Chêne by jumping over
the wrought-iron fence that enclosed the property. He roamed
through the neighborhood until he crawled through an open
window and into the bedroom of an elderly neighbor woman.
Panicked, she called the police, and they took the cheetah to
the zoo. Although Joséphine tried to convince the officers she
would keep Chiquita at home, they refused to release the now
full-grown animal that had developed a reputation for clawing
at women's legs. At first, Joséphine visited the cheetah at the
small zoo where he was housed, but the visits tapered off. In
later years, if someone asked about him, she said that Chiquita
had died.

In 1932, Joséphine opened in the show *La Joie de Paris,* or *The
Joy of Paris*, a new revue at the Casino. In October she made
an appearance in London, but it was not a big success. While
there, she achieved another first when she went to a studio at
16 Portland Place and made an appearance on a new medium:
television.

Following her television debut, she went on another tour all
over Europe and briefly into Africa and Asia before returning to
France to perform in a film written especially for her. *Zouzou,*

Joséphine broadcasting at the experimental Baird television studio, 16 Portland Place, London, in October 1931.
© BBC/Corbis

a light romantic comedy, was produced in the summer of 1934. Although the film had a weak plot, audiences praised Joséphine's natural performance in her first talking movie. Pepito worked hard to publicize it. He had stickers printed that said "Josephine Baker is *Zouzou.*" He then sent salesmen out into the city to talk banana sellers into allowing a sticker to be placed on each banana. It worked, and the success of *Zouzou*, plus the continued sales of her endorsed products, especially the hair preparation Bakerfix, caused Joséphine to be named the richest black woman in the world.

Though Joséphine's professional life was doing well, her family life was falling apart. In 1934, her stepfather, Arthur Martin, committed suicide in the mental hospital where he had been committed several years earlier due to his uncontrollable outbursts of rage. Although Joséphine had kept in touch with her family through letters and money she sent, news of her stepfather's death was a tragic reminder of the life she had escaped.

After her performance in *Zouzou*, Joséphine received an offer to star in the revival of *La Créole*, an operetta from 1875. She was uncertain about what to do when she first heard the music— it was not what she usually sang. But the more she listened, the better she liked the melodies, and she agreed to perform as the opera's lead. The story features a Jamaican girl seduced by a French sailor who later abandons her. She searches until she finds him, and the two are reunited. As Joséphine rehearsed the operetta, she became excited about the chance to appear in legitimate theater. Up to that point, she had performed only in music halls. She was proud that after just 10 years in the country, she was acting with an all-French cast in a role in which she spoke and sang in French.

The play opened on December 15, 1934, and it was unanimously praised by critics. The show ran for months, making it Joséphine's biggest artistic success in that decade. From the operetta she moved on to another film, *Princesse Tam-Tam*. Joséphine stars as Alwina, a free-spirited goatherder from Tunisia, who meets a visiting French novelist. Desperate to regain his wife's wandering attention, the novelist invites Alwina to return to Paris with him and to pose as the mysterious Princess Tam-Tam. Through a series of misadventures and twists of fate, the novelist and his wife are reunited, and Alwina returns to Tunisia.

After she met her film commitments, Joséphine and Pepito talked about going to America. She had mixed emotions, wondering if she could dazzle Broadway the way she had captured Paris. But when a friend asked her how she felt about returning to the United States, Joséphine told her, "I'm so excited. I'm all puffed up like a frog. Pepito's heard that New York is a wonderful place, all new and friendly. But I'm afraid I'll feel like a stranger. I don't know what will happen."

6

Storms of Life

JOSÉPHINE PROVED HERSELF IN FRANCE in the 10 years since she had arrived with the *Revue Nègre*. Now she wanted to impress her fellow countrymen. Pepito arranged for Joséphine to appear in the 1936 Ziegfeld Follies at a salary of $1,500 a week.

Joséphine was the first and last black woman to appear with the Ziegfeld Follies. In September, Joséphine and Pepito sailed for New York on the luxurious *Normandie*, whose passengers included Joséphine's friend Colette. Excitement and fear alternated in Joséphine's mind. When she debarked in New York, a swarm of reporters and photographers greeted her. Then, she and Pepito found Miki Sawada, the wife of the Japanese consul to the United States, waiting for them. Joséphine and Miki had met at a party in Paris four years earlier. The two immediately felt a kinship, and the Sawadas became frequent weekend visitors at Joséphine's home. Miki often accompanied Joséphine on her visits to the orphanage near Le Beau Chêne. In 1935, Mr. Sawada was transferred to the United States, so when Miki heard that Joséphine was going to America, she offered to meet her at the harbor.

Singer and dancer Joséphine Baker poses with daisies in the 1936 Ziegfeld Follies program.
© *John Springer Collection/CORBIS*

ZIEGFELD FOLLIES

The first Ziegfeld Follies, put on in July 1907, was a lavish production designed after the Folies Bergère of Paris. The show, featuring a chorus line of 50 beautiful women, opened at Jardin de Paris, a rooftop garden above the New York Theater. The Ziegfeld Follies launched the careers of many well-known names from the 1900s—performer Eddie Cantor, black comedian Bert Williams, comedienne Fanny Brice, actor Will Rogers, composer Irving Berlin, and actress Billie Burke, later known for her role as the good witch Glinda in *The Wizard of Oz*.

Showgirls who went on to become stars in their own right included Barbara Stanwyck, Paulette Goddard, and Gypsy Rose Lee. The show also presented the first run of popular songs like "Ol' Man River" and "Shine On, Harvest Moon." The Follies were an annual production from 1909 to 1931, except for three years in the late 1920s. The end of the Follies productions was closely followed by the death of their creator, Florenz Ziegfeld Jr., on July 22, 1932. The next year, his widow revived the Follies, and periodic shows were presented until 1957.

The three headed to Hotel St. Moritz where Pepito had made reservations. But when they tried to register, the manager informed them that Joséphine could not stay there because of her race: he feared her presence might offend the hotel's Southern guests. The usually devoted Pepito remained at the St. Moritz and left Joséphine to travel around the city with Mrs. Sawada, looking for another hotel willing to house an African American woman. Pepito's abandonment of Joséphine while she found a place to stay signaled the breakdown of their relationship. After she was refused accommodations everywhere she inquired, Joséphine accepted the Sawadas' offer to stay in their studio. Upon arriving, she sank to the floor and huddled in a corner where she wept and wept in humiliation. Miki could not believe this was the same woman she had seen in Europe, standing triumphant on the stage as the audience showered her with flowers.

After recovering from her initial upset, Joséphine settled into the studio. While she waited for the Follies rehearsals to begin, she traveled to Chicago to meet her husband, Willie Baker, with whom she had had no direct contact. She initiated divorce proceedings in 1928, but they were cancelled for lack of activity. One time during their separation, she had written inviting him to visit her in France; he declined. Willie seemed willing to wait for her return. Now, after 16 years of marriage, Joséphine arranged for their divorce. Willie offered no objections and even said he would take her back if she later wanted him.

From Chicago, Joséphine went to St. Louis to visit her family, which by now was much smaller due to the deaths of her sister Willie Mae, Grandma McDonald, and her stepfather, Arthur Martin. Joséphine spent five days with her family. "She just slept and ate, that's all," said her brother Richard. "She slept with our grandmother, who was surrounded by monkeys and parakeets." Joséphine's young nephew further revealed, "My grandmother's apartment was on the second floor, and you had to go downstairs to the outdoor toilet. Joséphine Baker had to go outside! She had to ask me to get her a basin of water so she could wash up because there was no bathroom."

While in St. Louis, Joséphine took her mother to look for a house in the best neighborhood occupied by blacks. Carrie found a white stone cottage she liked but refused to accept her daughter's offer to pay $20,000 in cash for it. Carrie couldn't believe anyone legitimately had that much money.

Joséphine returned to New York to begin practice for the Ziegfeld Follies. There was such a huge cast that rehearsals were held in four different theaters. Joséphine saw only those acts that practiced in her theater, and those in other theaters did not see her until the show went on the road to Philadelphia before its formal opening in New York. She had been told she would have equal billing with the Follies star, Fanny Brice, but Joséphine participated in only three acts compared to Fanny's seven. Audiences and newspaper reporters did not like Joséphine's performance, including exotic dances and a difficult song that covered two octaves. She was the only one of the stars the critics panned.

The New York performances opened at the Winter Garden Theatre on April 20, 1936. On the ground floor, the building housed the Plantation Theater Restaurant, where Joséphine had worked as a teenager and where Caroline Reagan had first hired her to go to France. When the New York Follies opened, Joséphine received criticism similar to that on the road. The main complaint was that she could not be heard in the huge Garden. One *New York Times* critic claimed,

After her cyclonic career abroad, Joséphine Baker has become a celebrity who offers her presence instead of her talent. . . . Her singing voice is only a squeak in the dark and her dancing is only the pain of an artist. Miss Baker has refined her talent until there is nothing left of it.

To offset these negative attacks, Pepito hired people to sit among the theater audience and clap wildly whenever Joséphine appeared on the stage. The diversion did not fool the audience or columnist Walter Winchell, with whom she was destined to cross swords in the future. He wrote, "Critics aren't fooled by noise."

The Follies experience was the worst failure of Joséphine's career. As she often did when things did not go well, Joséphine blamed Pepito. She chastised him for not arranging more favorable contract terms so that she would have better roles, better billing, and a more prominent place in the show. This was all Pepito could take. He was ill and decided to return to France. Neither of them was aware he was dying of cancer, so he left Joséphine on her own in the United States.

To compensate for the failure onstage, Joséphine opened Chez Joséphine, a nightclub on East 54th Street in New York. Every night when the Follies ended at 10:30 PM, she went to Chez Joséphine, where she performed the kind of acts with which she was comfortable. On opening night, she held a little pig and fed it using a baby bottle. To the delight of her audiences, she sang in both French and English. The smaller room fit her light voice, and this time the press was kinder to her. In May, Joséphine's fortune turned. The lead Follies star, Fanny Brice, became ill, and the show shut down until she could recover. Cast members had the choice of receiving a stipend and waiting for the show's reopening, or they could cancel their contract. Joséphine chose the latter—she was free. In later years she refused to talk about her experience with the Follies, one of the main disappointments in her life.

Deep sadness greeted her that spring when she received word that Pepito had died due to kidney cancer. In his will he left everything to Joséphine. Knowing her reckless spending habits, he told a friend she would need every penny of it.

A Frenchman saved Joséphine from despair. One night before the Follies closed, Paul Derval, the producer at the Folies Bergère, came to visit her in her dressing room. He told her Paris planned another colonial exposition in 1937 and that the Folies would be playing while all the tourists were in town. He invited her to star in his new revue called *En Super Folies*. After Paul made the offer, Joséphine screamed when he started to sit down on a white satin chair. He thought she was getting ready to demand more money, but actually she didn't want him to sit on her Chihuahua.

Although performing in the Folie would be a step backward in her career, Joséphine needed a job. Pepito was no longer around to arrange contracts for her, plus she missed his companionship. She was lonely and longed for a husband and a family. She had known many Frenchmen who were willing to be her lover, but none wanted to marry her. Then she met Jean Lion. The 27-year-old sugar broker was wealthy, handsome, and athletic. He was also Jewish, an ethnic group persecuted in the 1930s. Unlike many other Frenchmen, he had already dealt with prejudice, and was undeterred by Joséphine's skin color. He was enthralled by Joséphine and pursued her with an intensive courtship. On her 31st birthday, he wrote:

> *Cherie*, I am not going to speak of love here because you know how I feel about you. But I do want to express my happiness at having been with you today along with dear friends and some of my family, who I know would be happy to become part of yours . . . I hope for many more birthdays together. All of them perhaps? From your Jean, with all his love.

Jean greatly exaggerated his parents' desire to form a relationship with Joséphine. In fact, his parents and most of his friends were horrified at the thought of a marriage between the two. Yet Jean ignored their objections because he believed Joséphine's popularity would be an asset to his budding political career. The two married five months later on November 30, 1937, in the village where Jean's parents lived. By that time, his parents had reluctantly accepted Joséphine as their new daughter-in-law. Meanwhile, Joséphine renounced her American citizenship and became a French citizen with the vows she took.

The couple lived at Le Beau Chêne but seldom saw each other since his business schedule and her Folies performances did not coincide. Her dearest wish was to have a baby, and 14 months after the couple wed, Joséphine became pregnant. Just as with her first pregnancy, she began to knit baby clothes. When she had a miscarriage, the clothes disappeared. Not long after that, and primarily due to their long periods apart from each other, she and Jean separated. However, their divorce was not granted until 1941, which meant that in the interim, Joséphine was a member of two groups—blacks and Jews—who were persecuted by the Nazis as World War II spread throughout Europe.

During this period of separation and divorce, Joséphine met Frida Kahlo, a talented Mexican painter who had come to Paris in 1939 for an exhibition of her art, mostly self-portraits. The two were introduced at a nightclub after Joséphine sang and were immediately attracted to each other. Both were strong, talented women who did not let public opinion sway their actions. Both had overcome hardships in their youth. Frida had polio, and at age 18, she had been in a horrible car accident resulting in injuries that required her to stay in bed for over a year. As they shared life stories, they also revealed that they were bisexual. Eventually, the two women became lovers.

At the Casino de Paris, Henri Varna had plans to feature Joséphine in a new revue that had a Brazilian setting. But Henri's plans for the revue were put on hold when France and Britain declared war against Germany on September 3, 1939, following

Germany's attack on Poland, with whom France had a defense agreement. The French expected the Germans to try to cross their borders immediately and placed soldiers all along the Maginot Line, a vast fortification spread along the French-German border. Nine months passed, and nothing happened. People began to call it the "phony war," and the bored troops longed for entertainment. With the declaration of war, Henri decided it was no longer appropriate to present the new revue and sought a program to replace it. The result was *Paris/London*, a two-part show filled with singing and dancing, and starring Joséphine and Maurice Chevalier, a 51-year-old French actor.

Before the show opened at the Casino, Henri decided to try it out with performances for the soldiers.

Joséphine singing for British troops on leave from combat during World War II. © *Hulton-Deutsch Collection/CORBIS*

Maurice insisted that he be the last to perform—a position reserved for the star of a show. Joséphine gave in with little argument and went first. But she was so popular with the young men that they called her back for encore after encore. When Maurice got to perform, there was time for only a few numbers because the soldiers had to observe curfew. He was furious and threatened to leave the show. Although he stayed, he warned Joséphine that rivals could be dangerous. When later asked about Maurice, her only response was, "He is a great artist but a small man." Back at the Casino, they agreed on an intermission that would divide the show exactly in half to avoid any future conflicts.

Around the same time that *Paris/London* was gaining popularity, Jacques Abtey, the 33-year-old head of military counterintelligence in Paris, was looking for people whose lifestyles allowed them to move about freely and to gather information at the parties and receptions they attended. These people also had to be willing to work without pay. Daniel, the older brother of Joséphine's agent, Félix Marouani (whom she hired after Pepito's death), recommended her to Jacques. At first Jacques refused to consider Joséphine, fearing she would be like the famous double agent Mata Hari, who was also a dancer.

While Jacques wavered about what to do, the Germans moved closer to Paris, causing a mass exodus from the city in early June 1940. A few months earlier, Joséphine had rented Chateau des Milandes, a huge estate 300 miles to the south. She had prepared to flee there by storing gasoline in champagne bottles, knowing that none would be available on the road. With the Germans approaching, she loaded as many possessions as she could into her Packard and left Paris, along with her maid Paulette, a Belgian refugee couple, and three of her dogs. Their motley crew joined the line of cars, vans, bicycles, motorcycles,

MATA HARI

Mata Hari, born Margaretha Geertruida Zelle, grew into a spoiled young woman who married a captain 22 years her senior. Her extravagant spending marked their turbulent marriage. When they divorced, the captain notified creditors that he would no longer be responsible for her debts. Margaretha turned to seducing wealthy men to support her; one of them encouraged her to go onstage. Because of her uninhibited movements and her willingness to perform almost naked, she became a hit with Parisian audiences, and she adopted the stage name Mata Hari, meaning "eye of the day" or "dawn."

French authorities later hired Margaretha to spy on the Germans in occupied Belgium during World War I. While there, she had an affair with a German officer. Although she claimed never to have shared any French secrets with him, her actions aroused suspicion. She was arrested and taken before a French military court. At her trial, no one produced any documents that she might have passed to the enemy, and most of the accusations against her were pure speculation. Nevertheless, the tribunal found her guilty and sentenced her to death by firing squad. On the day of her execution, 41-year-old Mata Hari refused to be tied to a stake or to wear a blindfold—instead she faced her executioners eye-to-eye as 12 soldiers raised their rifles and fired simultaneously. Despite the doubt about her guilt, her name has gone down in history as a seductive spy.

pushcarts, and every other kind of transport leaving Paris. Joséphine did not see the city again for four years.

On June 14, the Germans captured Paris. They found only
700,000 people of the city's five million population still there.
Those who had remained put up no resistance. They recalled
the terrible losses from World War I and believed occupation
was preferable to more bloodshed. France and Germany signed
an armistice dividing France into two parts: northern and
southern. The Germans controlled the northern portion, and
the French retained control of the southern section known as
Vichy France. By July 15, most of the Parisian businesses and
entertainment centers had reopened, but there were changes as
the Germans took over the city. The Nazi swastika flew over the
Arc de Triomphe, the monument dedicated to those who fought
for France, especially in the Napoleonic Wars. Goose-stepping
soldiers patrolled the Champs-Élysées, a famous avenue used for
all types of French celebrations. Restaurant menus were printed
in German, and the city was no longer safe for Jewish or black
people, two groups whom the Germans wished to eliminate.

While Paris adjusted to the new order, Jacques Abtey decided
to meet Joséphine to determine if she could act as a possible
counterintelligence agent. He traveled to Chateau des Milandes, where he expected to find a sophisticated woman dressed
in the height of fashion. Instead he found Joséphine wearing
old clothes and walking around the grounds collecting snails to
feed the ducks. After they had talked for a while, he decided she
had good connections that could provide opportunities for her
to learn military secrets. Joséphine told him, "France made me
what I am. I will be grateful forever. The people of Paris have
given me everything. They have given me their hearts, and I
have given them mine. I am ready, captain, to give them my life.
You can use me as you wish."

Joséphine recognized that the Nazis were waging a racist war. She had waited a long time to fight against racism and was glad to join the effort against Nazi Germany. With this assurance of her love for and loyalty to France, Jacques invited her to become a spy.

Joséphine added intelligence assignments to her already busy schedule, and she entered the new role with the same energy and enthusiasm that she brought to any part she played. One of her first jobs was at a refugee center where she welcomed people fleeing from the Germans who had overtaken Belgium. In addition to welcoming the displaced, she identified spies. She became so diligent at the task that she assumed any young blond man was a German. For a while she kept Jacques busy interviewing innocent Belgians.

Jacques cautioned her that any French sympathizer could be a secret Nazi, but Joséphine shrugged off his warnings and accepted invitations to numerous diplomatic functions. Everyone knew her and wanted to see her. Her connections and enormous popularity gave her the perfect cover to collect information about German troop movements and activity at harbors and airfields. Joséphine wrote the overheard information along her arms and in the palms of her hands. She laughed off the potential danger, believing no one would suspect her of being a spy . . . and she was right.

While the remaining Parisians resumed their daily lives, one man refused to accept the German occupation. His name was General Charles de Gaulle, and he attempted to organize a resistance by making radio broadcasts from England, where he had fled. He begged all who could make their way to London to join him. Again, memories of the tragedies of World War I stopped most people from joining his rebellion, and only about 2 percent came. One of those people who answered de Gaulle's call to arms was Jacques Abtey, who decided to defect from the French army and join de Gaulle's efforts. His only problem was how to get to London from France.

Jacques had classified documents that he wanted to get to London. He first needed to establish contact with Portugal, a neutral country where the British had representatives to whom these sensitive documents could be safely delivered. Since the United States was also still neutral, Jacques disguised himself as an American and went by the name Jack Sanders. Knowing that Joséphine performed in Portugal from time to time, he went to see if she had contacts there to help him.

By then, Joséphine realized she needed to get out of France. A few days earlier, a group of German soldiers had appeared at Chateau des Milandes, where she was secretly housing a number of potential Resistance fighters. The senior officer told her, "We are informed, madame, that you are hiding weapons in your château. What have you to say to that?" Her response charmed them and they left without entering: "I think that *monsieur l'officier* cannot be serious. It is true that I had Red Indian grandparents, but they hung up their tomahawks quite a while ago now, and the only dance I've never taken part in is the war dance." Despite her cool demeanor, the incident frightened her; the time for her to move on had come.

Jacques had already contacted Charles de Gaulle, who accepted the pair into the Free French movement. Shortly thereafter, they were instructed to go to Lisbon, the capital of Portugal. The neutral city had become the crossroads of international intelligence as agents for both sides spied on each other. From Portugal, information could be sent to London. Joséphine agreed to go to Portugal with Jacques, who pretended to be her secretary/assistant. He already had 52 pieces of secret information about German installations and troop movements. Joséphine risked her safety by having this secret information written in invisible ink on her sheet music.

7

Joséphine's Challenges

PORTUGAL WELCOMED JOSÉPHINE with invitations to diplomatic parties at the British, Belgian, and French embassies. As she moved from one ambassador to another, she listened for information to help the Resistance. Then she went back to her hotel room and made careful notes on slips of paper that she pinned to her underwear. She felt confident that no one would strip-search her.

Obeying instructions sent by de Gaulle, Joséphine returned to Marseille, a part of Vichy France not under German control at that time. Although she had earlier vowed not to perform in France until all Germans were gone, Joséphine was short on cash, so she decided to go onstage again. She and Frédéric Rey, with whom she had danced in the *En Super Folies*, revived the operetta *La Créole* at the Théâtre de l'Opéra. In a flurry of activity, Joséphine selected a cast, found costumes, and opened the show on Christmas Eve 1940, all within the space of two weeks.

While she continued performing in the opera through the month of January, Jacques Abtey got word that Germany would

FRENCH RESISTANCE, WORLD WAR II

Most French citizens were shocked when France surrendered to Germany in early 1940. They believed the government had let them down. Citizens of varying political backgrounds joined together to fight their common enemy: the Germans. Germany, Japan, and Italy were known as the Axis powers. Members of the Allied resistance movement, made up of many cells of armed men and women, were from the United States, Great Britain, Russia, and France. The resistance also developed an alliance with the British government, which supplied the French with equipment and trained agents. In return, the French provided the British with vital intelligence reports.

From London, Charles de Gaulle used the airwaves to encourage his French countrymen to resist the Germans. He set up a central intelligence agency that worked cooperatively with a similar group in England. By 1943, there were 100,000 members of the various French resistance groups, gathering intelligence, destroying railways to stop the German movement, and assisting downed Allied pilots to escape. By the time of the Normandy invasion in June 1944, the French Resistance had played an important role in the Allies' success.

soon occupy all of France. He went to Marseille to warn Joséphine. The two made plans to travel to a French colony in North Africa, where they could continue to support the Resistance.

Before Joséphine left France, she sent for several of her animals to be brought from Chateau des Milandes: three monkeys, two white mice, a Great Dane named Bonzo, and a hamster. She couldn't bear to leave the rest of her pets behind, but she believed bringing several on her voyage would be a good cover—no one was likely to suspect her of espionage if she were traveling with a menagerie.

By the end of January 1941, Joséphine and Jacques reached the French colony of Algiers but soon moved on to Casablanca, a port city in Morocco. There they connected with the Free French Forces and became part of the Resistance network. The two also became lovers, and their relationship lasted for five years. While working for the Resistance, Joséphine moved freely from North Africa to Spain to Portugal, all the while performing to enthusiastic audiences.

On one of her return trips to Casablanca, Joséphine consulted a gynecologist because she so desperately wanted to have a baby. The doctor performed several treatments, which should have been followed by several days of rest. Instead, the doctor released her to go on the 250-mile trip to Marrakesh, where Jacques was staying. Two days later, she doubled over with terrible stomach pains as she and Jacques strolled around the little town. He got her back to their quarters and put her to bed, but then she developed a high fever. No ambulance was available to get her back to the doctor in Casablanca, so Jacques hired a station wagon to transport her. He rushed her to a private clinic owned by Dr. Henri Comte. Joséphine entered Dr. Comte's facility in June 1941 and did not leave until December 1942.

There was never an official statement about why Joséphine first came to the clinic. However, a worker there said the doctor performed a hysterectomy, and after that Joséphine developed first peritonitis and then septicaemia, a blood infection that was usually fatal in the days before penicillin was available. The infections built up scar tissue that caused intestinal blockage, requiring Joséphine to undergo even more surgery. Joséphine had so many operations during her stay that she finally jokingly asked her doctors: "Why don't you just put a zipper in? It would be so much easier." In addition to all of the medical issues, she, along with Jacques, mourned the fact that she would never be able to give birth to a baby.

As she recovered from her medical procedures, Joséphine's clinic room became a rendezvous point for supporters of the French Resistance. Visitors came daily—friends, ambassadors, and American diplomats. There was much discussion about when the United States would enter the war. The Japanese bombing of Pearl Harbor on December 7, 1941, ended the speculation. Three days later, both Germany and Italy declared war on the United States. Hungary and Bulgaria did the same on December 13, 1941.

Because Joséphine had not been seen in public for some time, in early November 1942, the United Press International issued the incorrect information that she had died. Newspapers around the world proclaimed her death in big headlines. The first assignment for a new reporter at the *Chicago Defender* was to write the performer's obituary. That man was Langston Hughes, who in future years would become one of America's greatest poets. He wrote that Joséphine was "as much a victim of Hitler as the soldiers, who fall today in Africa fighting his armies. The Aryans drove Joséphine away from her beloved Paris." Back in the United States, Joséphine's little sister

Margaret read in the newspaper that her sister was dead. She raced to tell her mother, who replied, "Tumpy ain't dead." She was right.

When Joséphine first heard a report of her death, she was 5,000 miles away at the palace of Mohamed Menebhi near the border of North Africa and the Sahara Desert. Reclining on a pile of pillows, surrounded by flowering trees, she talked to Ollie Stewart of the *Afro-American*. She told him, "There has been a slight error, I'm much too busy to die."

Gradually, Joséphine grew stronger and could move about the clinic room and go out on the balcony. She was there on November 8, 1942, when American troops landed near Casablanca as part of the Allied invasion of North Africa. Despite her sometimes hostile feelings toward her home country, when she saw the soldiers marching through the streets, Joséphine rejoiced: "That's the Americans for you. Europe doesn't know their force or their will. They'll win the war for us."

Seeing her countrymen gave Joséphine new energy, and in December, after 19 months in the clinic, she returned to Marrakesh to continue her convalescence. Shortly after arrival, she developed a bad case of parathyroid disease, which affected her body's calcium levels. Joséphine became depressed, and feared she might never get well.

While she dealt with this new health problem, the American soldiers in Casablanca grumbled about having nothing to do. They could not date the local young women because of a law preventing their socializing together. At that time, United States forces were still segregated, and this led to tension between the black and white GIs. The Red Cross opened the Liberty Club, where both black and white soldiers could enjoy themselves, but only at separate times. Sydney Williams, the director of the club, needed entertainment for the men. He learned that

Joséphine was in Marrakesh. Not knowing how ill she had been, he invited her to perform for the troops.

Joséphine wasn't sure what to do. She was still recovering from her multiple surgeries and illnesses. Her stomach was covered with unhealed surgical scars, and her legs looked like toothpicks. When she stood up, she saw spots dance before her eyes. Despite these physical problems, she accepted the invitation on the condition that both races must be allowed to sit together. She argued: "We've got to show that blacks and whites are treated equally in the American army or else what's the point of waging war on Hitler?" The club yielded to her extraordinary demand.

Joséphine explained: "My program included two American songs—a Negro lullaby to prove I hadn't forgotten my origins and a Gershwin tune to show the poetry of the American soul— then 'J'ai Deux Amours' to emphasize that I was French now and that France was a land of liberty. For this reason she must be returned to her people." In her first performance, Joséphine entered the club by walking down a staircase as she sang her theme song, "J'ai Deux Amours," backed by a band of army musicians. The audience responded with emotion. From that time on, she grew stronger, performing night after night for the soldiers. As she did, she began the second part of her wartime career: entertaining American, French, and British troops. Over the next two and a half years, she made numerous difficult tours across the scorching North African desert, traveling in jeeps, trucks, and any other vehicle that could move her from one place to the other. Joséphine and her companions traveled mostly by jeep, and at night they slept on the ground near their vehicles to avoid land mines. Heat blasted them during the day, and in the darkness, cold penetrated their bodies. They ate only what they could carry—often canned tuna fish.

Joséphine performed several times a day in front of thousands of soldiers. She filled their heads with dreams of romance and of a world without war, but she battled her own realization that many of the young men for whom she performed would die. She often knew which troops were headed for battle before they did. As she observed their energy and enthusiasm at her shows, she mourned their deaths to come. Entertaining the troops also brought Joséphine into close contact with black Americans serving in the army, most of whom served as construction workers, cooks, or food servers. Of the half million African Americans in the United States Army, only 5 percent were in combat units. Joséphine learned from them how widespread racial discrimination still was in the United States. She promised the black soldiers that when the war was over, she would return to her native country to help fight segregation.

In Algiers in the winter of 1943, Joséphine met Charles de Gaulle for the first time. After she gave a benefit for the Free French Forces, de Gaulle presented her a tiny gold Croix de Lorraine, or Cross of Lorraine, the emblem to represent that group. Despite the fabulous jewels Joséphine had worn in her life, she treasured the small gold cross more than any of those. The fact that she loved the Croix de Lorraine so deeply made her later decision to auction it off in a fundraising effort for the Free French Forces even more poignant. Because of her success with the fundraising, she was awarded the honorary rank of sublieutenant in the Ladies' Auxiliary of the French Air Force.

Shortly thereafter, on June 6, 1944, Allied troops invaded Normandy in an attack later known as D-Day.

From Normandy, the Allied troops marched south to Paris, and after more than four years of Nazi occupation, Paris was liberated on August 26, 1944. General Dietrich von Choltitz, the German commander in the city, ignored an order by Adolf

D-DAY

Although many historians have offered suggestions for what the *D* in D-Day represents, it is simply the army's way of reserving a particular day for a certain activity until the actual date can be determined. This also prevents the enemy from learning of the exact timing of Allied plans.

The most famous D-Day was on June 6, 1944, when Allied troops invaded the French coast in the Normandy region. It was the biggest amphibious military assault (meaning it took place on land and in water) in history, and the attack required unprecedented planning, coordination, and boldness. The attack combined 150,000 Allied soldiers, 5,000 ships, 30,000 vehicles, 13,000 parachutists, and 300 planes dropping 3,000 bombs. By the end of the day, 9,000 Allied soldiers were dead or wounded, but 100,000 had made it ashore and began securing the land taken from the enemy in order to launch other attacks.

Hitler to blow up landmarks and burn the city to the ground rather than allow it to be liberated. Instead, Choltitz signed a formal cease-fire agreement, and General Charles de Gaulle led his Free French troops in a triumphant march down the Champs-Élysées. Two months later, Joséphine wore her military uniform when she returned to Paris, where citizens welcomed her with cheers and tossed flowers as she moved through the streets in a parade.

Joséphine Baker in uniform of Ladies' Auxiliary of French Air Force, an honorary title given to her for her service to France as a spy during World War II. © *Hulton-Deutsch Collection/CORBIS*

Despite the joy of coming home to a free France, Joséphine hated the fact the Nazis had lived in Le Beau Chêne, her home in Paris. Although they had left it in good condition, just the thought of the German occupancy saddened her. Of more concern, though, were the terrible conditions in which many of the French survivors, especially the elderly, lived. Their situations spurred her to pawn some more of her jewelry and buy meat, vegetables, and coal for them. She planned a tour to raise more money to help the war-weary people.

Around this time, Joséphine began to date 41-year-old Jo Bouillon, an orchestra leader from a musical French family. He and his musicians had accompanied Joséphine on some of her earlier wartime shows and now went with her on tours all over Europe during the last months of the war. One of their stops was on April 29, 1945, at the Adelphi Theater in London, where Joséphine gave a victory show to support the Allied troops. Nine days later, on May 7, 1945, Germany surrendered and the war in Europe ended. Joséphine returned to France for a celebration at the Théâtre des Champs-Élysées, where she had appeared 20 years earlier in her first show in France, *La Revue Nègre*.

Now that the war had ended, Joséphine wanted to demonstrate that people of all backgrounds and races could live together in harmony. She had first decided to focus on improving race relations while touring South America in 1929. She planned to live by example, and adopt many children of varying nationalities and races. But first she needed a place to raise the children and a husband to be a father to the young ones. For the first goal, she decided to buy Les Milandes, the castle-like, turreted château she had rented for years in the Dordogne region in the southwest corner of France. She sold Le Beau Chêne and one of her Paris apartments to help buy the property. In addition to living at Les Milandes with the children she planned to adopt, she wanted to turn Les Milandes into a tourist attraction.

In the meantime, Joséphine and her French Resistance companion Jacques Abtey were reunited during the 1945 Christmas season. While they visited, he suggested Joséphine and Jo Bouillon should make a tour through North Africa and Italy to perform for the troops still stationed there. Never able to refuse a request for the soldiers, Joséphine agreed, but since she didn't charge for military concerts, she found herself in financial straits: she still owed money on the Les Milandes property and had to pay for the travel expenses of the orchestra as well. She sold more of her jewelry to help foot these enormous costs.

Later that year, Joséphine experienced a recurrence of her intestinal problems and underwent surgery again. While she convalesced in the hospital in October 1946, the Free French government sent a delegation to award her the Médaille de la Résistance, or Medal of the Resistance, avec rosette, a medal created by Charles de Gaulle to recognize individuals who aided the Resistance during the war. De Gaulle's daughter, Madame Élisabeth de Boissieu, accompanied the delegation and brought a handwritten letter from her father.

Dear Mademoiselle Josephine Baker,

It is with all my heart and knowledge that I send you my sincere congratulations for the high distinction of the French Resistance which you have received.

Not long ago I fully appreciated the great services you have given in the most difficult moments.

After that I was more touched by the enthusiasm with which you have put your magnificent talent at the disposal of our Cause and for all who followed it.

My wife and I are expressing our fervent wishes for your rapid and complete recovery.

While I am waiting to have the honor of seeing you again, I beg you, dear Mademoiselle, to accept my respectful homages to which my wife wants to add her very sympathetic greetings.

C. de Gaulle

Wearing a bright red satin bed jacket and diamond earrings, Joséphine proudly received the medal while still recuperating in the hospital.

Once she recovered and returned to Les Milandes, she concentrated on turning the property into a tourist attraction. She hired 60 families in the surrounding village to install electricity, plumbing, and telephone service. They stocked the farm with 600 chickens plus cows, pigs, dogs, and peacocks. Joséphine had even more elaborate plans for the property—two hotels, three restaurants, a miniature golf course, courts for tennis, volleyball, and basketball, a wax museum of scenes from her life, stables, a bakery, a gas station, a post office, and a factory to produce foie gras, the liver paste for which the region was noted. While she worked to bring about these changes, she moved to the next phase of her dream—to marry a man who could become father to her soon-to-be-adopted children.

For that role she chose bandleader Jo Bouillon, whom she had been dating. Joséphine found him different from all the other men in her life. Jo was an educated man, having graduated from a prestigious music conservatory. His good business sense and love for nature would be assets in helping her oversee Les Milandes. Jo's friends and family discouraged the shy and quiet man from marrying the flamboyant and temperamental Joséphine, but he ignored them. On June 3, 1947, Joséphine's 41st

Joséphine Baker marrying her fourth husband, Jo Bouillon at a private chapel at Les Milandes on June 3, 1947, her 41st birthday. © *Bettmann/CORBIS*

birthday, the two wed, first in a civil ceremony, and again in a Roman Catholic rite. The church service surprised Joséphine's friends, who believed she had converted to Judaism when she married Jean Lion.

For her wedding, Joséphine wore a two-piece suit, a large pink straw hat with curled feathers, a white orchid corsage, and a gold belt. Almost all of Jo's family attended the wedding, and Pepito's sister Christine came with her family from Italy to represent the bride. The entire village attended the celebration at Les Milandes and ate the five-foot-tall wedding cake.

Before they married, Jo had made a commitment for his orchestra to play in Mexico, so the couple combined their honeymoon with live and radio performances in that country. A radio station in the United States picked up one of their on-air performances and invited the newly married couple to perform in a show at the Majestic Theatre in Boston. Apparently forgetting, or at least ignoring, Joséphine's previous experience performing in her home country 12 years ago, the couple accepted the invitation, not knowing the reception of their show in Boston would be humiliating.

8

Let My People Go

THE AMERICAN PRODUCERS OF *Paris Sings Again* rushed the preparation to open on December 25, 1947, so they could take advantage of Christmas crowds. Unfortunately, the show flopped for several reasons. The directors chose songs for Joséphine to sing that had no relationship to Paris. Critics seemed uninterested in her actual performance, and instead were more interested in her huge wardrobe of costumes and the expensive jewels that were so valuable that she was "under police guard while on the stage of the Majestic." There was a 33-carat emerald, a 16-carat sapphire, and a black diamond that gave off glints of red fire. But all the sparkling jewels in the world couldn't save the show: bad reviews caused sparse attendance, and the show closed only three weeks after its opening.

While she was in the United States, Joséphine visited her family in St. Louis and invited all of them to live with her at Les Milandes. She wanted them to see how successful she had become and what it was like to live in a place where blacks were treated equally to whites. Since Joséphine's last visit, her mother,

Carrie, had remarried. Her new husband, Tony Hudson, did not want to go to a country where people spoke a different language. In a show of independence, Carrie decided to go to France without him, and she never returned. Sister Margaret had also married, but her husband, Elmo Wallace, was ready to move. Brother Richard couldn't decide for sure—he said that he would think about it. He didn't join them in Paris for another four years.

The last thing Joséphine did before leaving the States was to accept an invitation to speak at the all-black Fisk University in Nashville, Tennessee. She talked about racial equality in North Africa and in France, and invited her audience to visit one of these places to experience life without prejudice. She told them that she had traveled incognito throughout the South, and it was her opinion that the racial situation was worse than ever. The university students responded positively to her message when she told them,

> I do not like people to say when they see an outstanding Negro performer 'Why, she is an exception.' There are few exceptions but lots of people with talent who never get the opportunity to display it. . . . We are the greatest race in the world, the Youth group should know this and they should be made to feel proud of our accomplishments. More is achieved by love than hate. Hate is the downfall of any race and nation.

Joséphine enjoyed the experience and decided she would like to do more public speaking. This speech became the catalyst for numerous appearances scheduled throughout the world in the coming years. She and Jo, as well as her family, left for France, but she determined to return to the United States soon to push for desegregation.

Upon reaching Les Milandes, Joséphine was glad to see some progress had been made in her absence in turning the property into a tourist attraction. But there was still much to do. While she waited for its completion, she returned to show business to earn money to pay for all of the renovations. On April 8, 1948, she and Jo opened a cabaret, Club des Champs-Élysées. A large, diverse crowd—including show-business celebrities, ambassadors, boxer Joe Louis, and Joséphine's one-time rival Mistinguett—attended the opening.

Joséphine at the Folies Bergère in 1949, wearing her headdress for a scene of courtly love, "Le Festin." © *Bettmann/CORBIS*

JOE LOUIS

Nicknamed the "Brown Bomber," Joe Louis grew up in the deep poverty and racial discrimination of the South. After his family moved to Detroit, he developed an interest in boxing. In 1933 he won the Golden Gloves as a light heavyweight and turned to professional boxing. One by one he defeated previous title holders until on June 19, 1936, when he went up against Max Schmeling, a protégé of Adolf Hitler. Although Max was the underdog, he defeated Louis in a surprise upset. Their rematch happened two years later, and Louis defeated Schmeling with a knockout.

Beginning in 1939, Louis began a 12-year reign as the world's heavyweight champion. In 1942 he left boxing to join the army, where he spent 14 months teaching physical education to soldiers. He did not return to the ring until 1946, when he successfully defended his title another four times. Despite the $5 million he earned in his lifetime, by the time he was 37 years old, he had no money remaining. His last fight, a defeat, was against Rocky Marciano, who sent Louis into the ropes in the eighth round. Louis still holds the record of having defended his title more times than any other fighter. He died at 66 years old, in 1981.

In 1949, Paul Derval invited Joséphine to appear again at the Folies Bergère in a show called *Féeries et Folies*, or *Enchantments and Foolishness*. This 15-letter title departed from Paul's usual insistence that his show's names always be exactly 13 letters to bring him good luck. Joséphine appeared in several skits, all based on fairy tales, and she also sang songs written especially for her. Her vocal performance was so well received that Columbia Records invited her to record several of the tunes.

Meanwhile, progress at Les Milandes was not going as well as it had while Joséphine was gone. She did not know how to manage people successfully, and her moodiness and temper tantrums upset the workers, who either quit or were fired. She and Jo disagreed about how to run the property: Joséphine managed by instinct, while Jo relied on facts. She ignored recommended planting times, so harvests never developed; she failed to ensure that the cows were milked regularly, but she became ecstatic about the fact that each animal had its name in neon lights over its stall. In contrast, Jo recognized his limited experience, and spent hours reading to gain the knowledge he needed to manage the farm. Their disagreements were inevitable.

After the Folies show closed in 1950, Joséphine toured Italy, where she had an audience with Pope Pius XII. For their meeting, she dressed all in white and wore a mantilla (scarf) over her dark hair, which was pulled into a severe chignon. Upon entering the Pope's presence, Joséphine knelt in respect. After the Pope pulled her to her feet and called her "my daughter," she told him about her plans to adopt children from many nationalities. He encouraged her by telling her, "There is a fundamental opposition between the church and racism. The church by universal definition professes the oneness of mankind." Then he blessed her. His blessing thrilled Joséphine because now she could mention the Pontiff's support in all of her publicity.

After the papal visit, she went on tour, spending six months in Mexico before taking her show to Havana, Cuba. Now that she was in her 40s, Joséphine no longer wanted to bare her body in skimpy costumes. Instead, she favored dresses with long, full skirts and tight waists, and she wore the latest fashions from the most notable French designers. News of her success in Cuba reached Florida, where Ned Schuyler, manager of a club in Miami called Copa City, invited her to perform. Joséphine saw the invitation as a chance to work for desegregation in the United States. However, when she informed Schuyler that she would not perform unless the seating was racially integrated, he tried to change her mind by offering her more and more money. The offers got bigger and bigger until they reached $10,000 extra for removing the restriction. Despite the enormous sum, Joséphine remained adamant that the audience include people of all races, and Schuyler finally relented. Actually, he personally believed in desegregation, and he helped Joséphine get a room at the Arlington Hotel, which had never before had a black guest. In addition, Joséphine had a white chauffeur to drive her car.

On opening night at the Copa City, only 11 African Americans, including fighter Joe Louis, showed up to see the show— most were afraid to cross the invisible boundary that separated the part of Miami in which they lived from the area occupied by the nightclub. Popular singer and actress Sophie Tucker introduced Joséphine, who was a tremendous hit. Joséphine told the first integrated audience: "This is the happiest moment of my life. I have waited 27 years for this night. Here I am in this city where I can perform for my people."

For every appearance, she filled the 750-person nightclub with an enthusiastic audience. Popular gossip columnist Walter

Winchell gave her a rave review in the January 17, 1951, issue of *New York Daily Mirror*: "Josephine Baker's applause [at Copa City] is the most deafening, prolonged, and sincere we ever heard in forty years of show-biz. A one-gal show, with exquisite gowns, charm, magic, and big-time zing. A star."

Joséphine was sincere about her desire to end segregation in the United States. When she accepted an offer to perform at the Roxy Club in New York at a salary of $20,000 per week, she used the daylight hours to involve herself in a variety of civil rights issues. The one that gained her the most publicity was her support of a black man named Willie McGee, who had been accused of raping a white woman while she lay in her bed with her small daughter. Many people, including Albert Einstein, rallied to Willie's defense and said that he had been framed. Although she could not stop his execution, Joséphine paid for his burial and stayed with his wife until Willie died. The next night, when she performed in Detroit, Michigan, Joséphine told the audience that she would perform that night but that her heart was saddened: "They have killed one of my people, Willie McGee. He was executed. I feel very deeply about it. I feel very deeply for my people, just as you feel very deeply about yours."

While in Philadelphia for five days, Joséphine met face-to-face with the heads of major corporations to urge them to hire black workers, and she challenged a large transit company's refusal to let blacks drive buses because the company claimed they weren't qualified. She wanted to know how it was possible that African Americans had driven buses throughout WWII but had now lost their ability to do so. The bus company president refused to budge, and a frustrated Joséphine walked out of the meeting. Later, at the Biltmore Hotel, she made a citizen's arrest when a man used an expletive against her race. In typical fashion, she made up a story on the spot, telling observers the arrest had been easy for her because her father had been a policeman.

Although her push for desegregation was not appreciated in many places, vast numbers of African Americans sought to honor her efforts. The NAACP (National Association for the Advancement of Colored People) declared May 20, 1951, Joséphine Baker Day in Harlem. When she contacted her husband Jo Bouillon about the honor, he was in France checking on the work at Les Milandes. She asked him to bring her two new Christian Dior outfits to wear for the celebration. Jo returned to the United States, carrying a white suit, a black ankle-length raw silk dress, and an off-white pleated gown. Joséphine had recently burned off much of her hair while applying a chemical straightening treatment, so he also brought a hat designed to fit over the artificial, foot-high, conical chignon she was wearing until her hair grew back. On her special day, Joséphine rode on the back of a cream-colored convertible as the 27-car motorcade moved slowly down 7th Avenue. It was reported that 100,000 people lined the street and hung from upstairs windows and fire escapes for a chance to see her. She got out in front of the Hotel Theresa at 7th Avenue and 125th Street to accept presentations from cultural and athletic groups including the American Legion and the Girl and Boy Scouts. That night, the mayor of New York, Vincent Impellitteri, gave a cocktail party in her honor. Five thousand people danced that evening in the Golden Gate Ballroom. Such a turnout encouraged Joséphine to continue her tour to push for civil rights. At that point in her life, it appeared nothing could stop her. She was wrong.

She was next scheduled to speak at the NAACP Convention in Atlanta, Georgia. When she tried to make reservations, she was turned down by three hotels based on her race before she decided to cancel her engagement altogether. The incident brought to light a law that stated that a hotel in Georgia could lose its license if it accommodated a black person's request for a room. The negative press coverage that followed Joséphine's event cancellation incited the wrath of the Ku Klux Klan, an extremist organization devoted to white supremacy, and Joséphine received threatening

Joséphine and Jo reading congratulatory telegrams after her 1951 performances at the Roxy Club in New York. © *Bettmann/ CORBIS*

letters in the mail. Joséphine returned for two weeks of performances at the Roxy Club in New York, where she grossed $55,000 from sold-out audiences every night.

Part of Joséphine's attraction was her fabulous $150,000 wardrobe. French designers gave her clothes because her wearing them provided wonderful advertising. Her clothes filled 6

WALTER WINCHELL

At one time Walter Winchell was America's most powerful journalist. He began his career by writing a gossip column for a New York newspaper, but he switched to radio in 1930. Two years later, he hosted a 15-minute radio show for which he developed his signature style—stories delivered at a rapid-fire pace in a staccato speaking style, and with the tapping of a telegraph key in the background. He created his own slang for the coast-to-coast audiences whom he addressed as Mr. and Mrs. America.

As his popularity grew, he held court at table 50 of the Stork Club, where he had access to the celebrities of the day. He associated with mob members and politicians. With a few sharp words, he ruined many careers. He let his emotion overrule his good judgment in the clash with Joséphine Baker, and his position was never the same again. By the time he died in 1972, little note was made of his passing. Nevertheless, Walter Winchell was inducted into the Radio Hall of Fame in 2004.

trunks, 48 suitcases, and 8 boxes containing 36 pairs of shoes and a few hats. A television poll named her the Best Dressed Woman of 1951.

Joséphine was riding high on the success of her recent shows until October 16, 1951, when she decided to meet some friends for dinner at the exclusive Stork Club on 53rd Street. That evening, Joséphine came face-to-face with the same unreasonable prejudice against which she had been fighting so hard. Roger Rico, who was starring in *South Pacific* at the time and was a frequent guest at the club, had invited her to dine with him and his wife. Around midnight, Joséphine and the Ricos entered the Stork Club and were seated. To get to their table, they passed the Cub Room, a special place set off by red velvet ropes and a watchful head waiter, for the most prestigious guests. Walter Winchell, the gossip columnist who had recently praised Joséphine's talent, sat at table 50, which was permanently reserved for him. The two waved casually at one another as Joséphine passed with her dining companions.

A waiter came to take their order. The Ricos wanted only drinks, but Joséphine was hungry after her show. She ordered steak, crab salad, and a bottle of French wine. After the waiter left their table, Joséphine noticed strange glances from the waitstaff. Her friends received their order, but she did not. Initially, she assumed it was because they had ordered only drinks. Rico tried to catch the attention of their waiter but was unsuccessful. Finally, after an hour, he raised his voice and demanded a waiter come to their table. Rico sent the waiter to find out where Joséphine's food was. The waiter returned with the news that the club was out of steak and crab meat salad and that they were still looking for the bottle of wine.

Joséphine was furious. She stormed away from the table and across the club to a telephone. She called Billy Rowe, the only black deputy commissioner in the New York City Police Department. She lodged a complaint about discrimination in the restaurant—a violation of the state Civil Rights Act and the State Alcoholic Beverage Control Law. When she went back to her table to join the Ricos, Walter Winchell was gone. Joséphine and the Ricos left the Stork Club to visit Walter White, executive director of the NAACP, and determine what legal action they could take in response to such blatant prejudice.

The next day, the papers carried the story of Joséphine's complaint against the Stork Club. The *Milwaukee Journal* quoted her as saying: "This is a terrible experience. . . . It is a snub to my color, to my people. It's not just something you can let drop. It is un-American. It is not fair to other Americans. I am consulting with my lawyers and I'm going to do something about it—not for Josephine Baker. I'm doing it for America."

At 7:00 PM, NAACP members picketed the club. For some reason Joséphine's wrath focused not on the club but on Walter Winchell, whom she claimed should have come to her aid because he was a good friend of the manager, Sherman Billingsley. Winchell claimed he was unaware of a problem and had left the club before Joséphine stormed out. On his next Sunday night broadcast, he said: "I am appalled at the agony and embarrassment caused Joséphine Baker in the Stork Club. But I am especially appalled at the efforts to involve me in an incident in which I had no part." Winchell, who was Jewish, resented being accused of discrimination, particularly since he had always prided himself on his lack of racial prejudices.

Joséphine picked the wrong person to focus on in her all-out battle against segregation. Thanks to his popular radio broadcasts, Winchell had the eyes and ears of Americans. He accused Joséphine of all sorts of treasonous activities. It was 1951, and a fear of Communism pervaded the nation. Winchell accused her of being a Communist. He found a 16-year-old article in which she had praised Italy's prime minister Benito Mussolini before his involvement in World War II. Winchell called Joséphine a Fascist. He even belittled her service for France during the war. He called her Josey-Phoney Baker.

Joséphine suffered the fallout of Winchell's baseless accusations. She had become a controversial figure, and one by one, theaters cancelled her scheduled appearances. With the cancellations, she lost the opportunity to become an American idol and to earn enough money to finish financing the work on Les Milandes. Sadly, Joséphine didn't understand much of the political rhetoric thrown at her since she lacked a formal education. Her activism was truly born of her simple desire to prove that all people could—and should—live together in harmony.

No one won the battle. The episode finally ended with the mayor's committee issuing its report that they had found nothing to support a charge of racial discrimination in regard to the Stork Club incident. Walter Winchell never regained his powerful position because the public and the media felt his accusations were unprofessional. Joséphine lost her opportunity to tour the United States and left for South America, where she would get in even deeper trouble.

9

In My Village

INSTEAD OF GOING DIRECTLY TO South America, Joséphine detoured through Cuba, ruled at that time by dictator Fulgencio Batista. Because he was half-black, Joséphine believed she could get him to support her world brotherhood crusade. However, she wasn't aware of Cuba's long history of racial discrimination against its black citizens. Upon her arrival in Havana, she quickly learned she had not escaped racial prejudice—two of the city's largest hotels refused her a room. When she arrived at the radio station where she was supposed to sing, police barred her entry. She at last found a small movie theater that, although it received threats, allowed her to sing. Each night she filled the auditorium.

One evening while she performed at the theater, Havana police searched her hotel rooms. After the show, the police arrested her on charges of supporting Communists, though the basis for that claim was not clear. After fingerprinting Joséphine and assigning her a criminal number, 0000492, the police

Grabbing attention in Havana with another new hairstyle with the help of hairdresser Jean Clement. © *Michael Ochs Archives/ Corbis*

demanded she sign a statement saying that she was working for Moscow. Joséphine, of course, refused. After intensive questioning, her captors took her photograph and led her to a hall where numerous pictures of "wanted people" were displayed. The police placed her picture on the wall and slapped a sign that said COMMUNIST under the photograph. They later claimed her arrest was a mistake and released her. Joséphine's only comment was to say that "everyone who believes in brotherhood has been accused of Communism."

In September 1952 Joséphine headed south to perform in Buenos Aires, Argentina. She originally planned to stay there for six weeks, but she became so enmeshed in the country's politics that she stayed for six months. Argentina was in mourning—two months earlier, its heroine, Eva "Evita" Perón, had died at an early age.

The poor people adored the woman who rose from the same kind of poverty that many of them endured. They saw her taking money from the rich to give it to them. What they didn't see was her stealing from the poor to make herself rich. They knew nothing about or simply ignored her $40,000 annual expenditures on Paris fashions and the Swiss bank accounts holding $20,000,000. After her early death from cervical cancer, she was further revered by Argentinians, many of whom went so far as to call her a saint.

Joséphine identified with Eva and was fascinated by her life story. Both women came from poverty-stricken childhoods and had little formal schooling. They both became singers. They both seemingly wanted to help the poor and downtrodden. At her first performance in Buenos Aires, Joséphine was delighted to learn that Eva's widowed husband, dictator Juan Domingo Perón, was in the audience. After the show, he sent one of his aides backstage to arrange a meeting with her. Joséphine

EVA PERÓN

Eva Perón, born Maria Eva Ibarguren, suffered from discrimination throughout her childhood because her parents were not married. She longed to be an actress, and after completing two years of high school, Eva went to Buenos Aires to pursue an acting career. When she discovered she had little acting ability but possessed an appealing voice, she began a successful career on radio. At a fundraising event for earthquake victims in 1944, she met Colonel Juan Perón, a fast-rising politician who was also a widower. The two were instantly attracted to each other, and within a few weeks she moved into his apartment. The two married one year later, in 1945, just after Juan was elected president of Argentina.

Eva, or Evita as she preferred to be called, was popular with the working-class people of Argentina. She felt close to them because of her own childhood struggles with poverty. Soon, Argentinians were clamoring for her to run for vice president. However, both she and her husband had numerous military and political opponents. Before she reached a decision, Evita was diagnosed with terminal cervical cancer, and she died at the age of 33. Almost a million Argentinians filled the streets to see her funeral procession. The 1979 musical *Evita* brought back to public awareness the life of this woman.

accepted the invitation, unaware of the damage Perón had done to his country. Under his leadership, Argentina had become a fascist state and a refuge for Nazi war criminals, but he had become popular with the masses through financial handouts. Since his wife's death, he had no idea about how to proceed because he had depended on her strong personality to guide his decision making.

The morning after he saw Joséphine perform, Perón sent a car to bring her to la Casa Rosada, the pink government mansion where he had his offices. When she met him, she noted the black band on the left upper arm of his suit coat worn to indicate that he was in mourning for his wife. She expressed her sympathy, and as they talked, he said that his wife had admired Joséphine and followed her career. After visiting with Joséphine a while, he realized that she had a strong character like his late wife, Eva. He invited her to speak to workers at a memorial rally for his wife. Joséphine agreed, but she did not think clearly about how her remarks would be interpreted in the United States, and she failed to recognize the significance of what she said. She spoke in flattering terms about Perón, a dictator whom the American government opposed. She praised him for what he had done for Argentina and at the same time criticized the United States for its ongoing racism. The Perón-backed newspapers loved everything she said and spread her speeches across the country.

An American newspaper picked up one of the Argentinian articles and distributed it in the United States, where even African Americans started to distance themselves from her, fearing that her remarks would hurt the civil rights movement. Her speeches in Argentina angered more Americans than had all of her previous civil rights work in the United States. The Justice Department publicly stated that if Joséphine Baker ever wanted to come back to the United States, "she would have to prove her right and worth." Perón took advantage of Joséphine's passion for social justice, and he encouraged her fiery speeches against the United States. Meanwhile, Joséphine used the platforms he provided to push her agenda of world brotherhood.

Perón also invited Joséphine to take over some of the duties of running the Eva Perón Foundation, which had been established by his late wife to build schools, hostels, and hospitals. In her new role for the foundation, she was scheduled to visit several hospitals, which Perón claimed were models for caring for the sick. But he didn't tell Joséphine that there were two sets of hospitals—those he showcased and the rest, the majority, which were in desperate need of personnel and supplies. He planned for her to see the well-run facilities, but Joséphine arranged her own tour based upon the buildings' locations.

Her independently arranged visit thus took her to see the deprived hospitals rather than the hospitals intended for public viewing. Most of the old and run-down buildings needed major repairs. They were understaffed and poorly equipped. Many did not have sufficient medications or even enough food for the patients. One of the institutions was a hospital for the mentally ill, where the people were treated like animals. An aide who accompanied Joséphine on her tour said, "They were rolling around the lawn in rags, eating their own filth."

Such conditions shocked Joséphine, who began to realize that the Perón regime was not what it appeared to be. She started listening to the people she met—hearing their tales of fear and of government oppression. She decided to go home. She was tired of both Americas—North and South—and longed to go back to France, to Jo, and to Les Milandes, where she planned to create her own world of unified brotherhood.

Upon her arrival at Les Milandes, Joséphine's first act was to try to turn it into a little kingdom with her as its reigning monarch. She had flags designed and she opened a fake post office with stamps printed to make Les Milandes seem like a country. The stamps could not be used for mail, of course, but the postmistress distributed them as gifts to tourists. Above the door to the château's theater was a neon-outlined silhouette of Joséphine. Her initials marked the wrought-iron gates to the property, and the swimming pool was in the shape of a J. The most flamboyant room in the hotel, La Chartreuse des Milandes, was called the Joséphine Room. Finally, there was Jorama, the wax museum that depicted scenes from her life, including one of a small girl dancing for her brothers and sisters in St. Louis and one of Joséphine's audience with the pope.

Although sometimes extravagantly generous to other people, Joséphine made sure that all of her family (except her mother, Carrie) contributed to the château's operation. Sister Margaret helped on the farm, and her husband, Elmo, maintained and rented paddleboats on a part of the Dordogne River that ran through the property. In 1952, Joséphine's brother Richard joined the rest of the family in France. Upon his arrival, Joséphine took him on a tour of Les Milandes. As they walked, she reminded him of how far they had come from the poverty of their St. Louis childhood: "Look what God has given us. To think of where we've come from and where we are today. I often think of the time when we were little kids and didn't have anything. I have often wished that we had this in America." Richard first served as his sister's chauffeur, but she soon built him a gas station with two pumps and a small garage. Located on the main road to Les Milandes, it soon became a profitable business.

Carrie was the only person who did not work and she never learned to speak French. Instead, she spent her days wearing a white linen dress and sitting in a rocking chair underneath a huge elm. Visitors who passed by her often took her picture, and she talked with those who spoke English. Although she accepted the generosity of her first child, she never understood why the public adored Joséphine.

It was time for Jo and Joséphine to start their demonstration of world brotherhood. Joséphine could have retired as a wealthy entertainer, but instead she focused on bringing children to Les Milandes. As she had told her old friend Miki Sawada, she wanted "to adopt five little two-year-old boys, a Japanese, a black from South Africa, an Indian from Peru, a Nordic child, and an Israelite [who] will live together like brothers." Since the children would not be blood-related, having only one gender would prevent problems when they became teenagers. Joséphine called the children her Rainbow Tribe. They would prove that all races and nationalities could live together in harmony. In the spring of 1954, Joséphine traveled to Japan for a speaking tour. She planned to adopt her first child while in that country.

Before leaving Les Milandes, she contacted Miki Sawada, who had become the director of the Elizabeth Saunders Home, an orphanage in a Tokyo suburb.

Upon her arrival at the Elizabeth Saunders Home, Joséphine walked through the building. All of the children looked alike to her, with their straight black hair and slanted eyes. She frequently stopped to play with one child or another. One little boy refused to leave her side. He was only 18 months old, but he did all he could to get her attention—hugging her and whispering words she could not understand. Miki told her they had named him Akio, or Autumn, because that was the time of the year when they found him. She said that he was Korean, he had been abandoned by his mother, and he was probably the child of an American soldier.

MIKI SAWADA

After World War II, many mixed-race children—born to Japanese women and American soldiers who were stationed in Japan during the occupation—were abandoned on the streets of Japan. Though Miki Sawada grew up in a wealthy Japanese family largely untouched by poverty, these abandoned children touched her heart. Since she was married to a diplomat, she had traveled widely, and had been impressed by the orphanages she visited while in London. Then, while living in America, Miki became very ill. During her stay in the hospital, a nurse told her the story of the Good Samaritan, and it had a tremendous impact on Miki. Miki became a Christian and decided she wanted to build an orphanage for children in Japan like the ones she had seen in England.

At first, Miki cared for children in her own home. Then the government took over all personal property, and the once-wealthy benefactor no longer had a place to raise them. Miki sold everything she had left and then sought donations. The first person to respond to her plea was a British nanny named Elizabeth Saunders, after whom Miki later named the orphanage when it was erected in 1948. Miki raised more than 2,000 orphans, and she treated them as if they were her own children. She died in 1980.

Joséphine decided he would be her first adopted child. As she left the orphanage with Akio, she walked down a long sidewalk. She saw a solemn baby sitting under a tree with a caretaker. The infant and Joséphine made eye contact that neither seemed capable of breaking. The caretaker explained that he loved being outside and cried when taken indoors. His name was Teruya; he was Shinto; and he had been born on July 15, 1953. Joséphine could not resist his sweet face, so she adopted him too.

She didn't inform Jo of the extra adoption until she stepped off the train in Paris with two bundles in her arms. He accepted the change in their plans, and they renamed Teruya "Janot" because it was easier for them to pronounce.

This trip established a pattern that Joséphine followed for years. As she made her way around the world, revisiting places where she had performed, she gathered more of her Rainbow Tribe. Next, she adopted Jari, a Scandinavian child with blue eyes and fair skin, from an orphanage in Helsinki. Adoptions in Finland were relatively easy because families could give a child to the government if they proved they could not afford to care for it. The government provided for such children for two months before sending them to foster care. The day that Joséphine visited the Helsinki orphanage, two-year-old Jari was scheduled to be moved into foster care. She paid the adoption fee to the Finnish government and left the orphanage with the chubby little boy in her arms.

The next tour took Joséphine to Bogotá, Colombia, in South America. There, the mother of eight black children approached her. The desperate woman said she could not afford to support so many children, and she asked Joséphine to adopt her youngest child, named Gustavio Valencia. Joséphine bought the family a small house and a garden in exchange for the child, and she promised to keep in touch with the mother and to bring the

Joséphine Baker and Jean-Claude, whom she and Jo adopted after she found the child starving in Paris. © *Bettmann/CORBIS*

boy back for a visit with his family. Joséphine did not keep her promise. Instead, she changed Gustavio's name to Luis, and she never told him about his previous life.

Joséphine had four children from three races and four religions, but she still didn't have a child from Peru. Instead she continued adopting other children. On her next trip into Paris, she found Jean-Claude in a French orphanage. This time, in addition to not seeking Jo's input, she used a nurse and a friend to carry the child to Les Milandes. Joséphine was not even there when the surprise for Jo arrived. When she came home, all she told her husband about the latest adoptee was that she couldn't leave behind a child who was starving. Jo reminded her to be conservative with her spending, especially because of the blow to their finances when her American tour that was supposed to bring in $200,000 had been cancelled. As usual, Joséphine paid little attention to Jo's warnings. She was determined to fill her life with the children she could not have naturally due to her earlier botched surgeries. "I suffered a lot because I couldn't have children of my own," she told a French reporter. "I felt inferior because of that."

While she waited to adopt a Peruvian Indian child, Joséphine focused on having a mixture of religions. She decided to search for a Jewish boy to go with the Catholic, Shinto, Buddhist, and Protestant religions already represented in her growing brood. Unlike the Finnish government, which had willingly allowed her to adopt a child, the Israeli government refused to let a child leave their country. Undeterred, Joséphine adopted a Jewish boy from France. At 10 months of age, the child she named Moïse became the youngest of the adopted children, of whom the oldest was four.

With six children to support, Joséphine needed to raise some money, so she went back to performing. She told the press: "I'll be fifty this year. It's time to retire. I want to say good bye to my people while I still have the physical strength." Her first farewell performance occurred at the Olympia Theatre in Paris on April 10, 1956. Joséphine dressed in a sophisticated gold-and-blue, strapless, floor-length dress and a red velvet coat lined with aquamarine satin. Her hair was curled in long ringlets that swept her shoulders. Top French actors from all the places she had performed presented a collage of scenes from her life. After Joséphine sang her favorite songs, she introduced a new theme song, an old folk tune with lyrics that described each of her adopted children. She called it "Dans Mon Village," or "In My Village." The French audiences, who still adored Joséphine, also loved the new song.

Life at Les Milandes was at the height of its success as well. Nearly 300,000 visitors toured the grounds annually. For a while, Joséphine seemed content devoting herself to her children and to the château. The family also had occasion to celebrate happy events: on her 50th birthday, her brother Richard married the Les Milandes postmistress. Meanwhile, news of her successful farewell show in Paris had spread, and other places where she had performed in earlier years begged her to perform. But the decision to take her show on the road was not an easy one because her children wanted her to stay home with them. Joséphine told a friend, "As I am leaving, [my daughter] will stretch herself out on the front hall floor and scream her head off. She says to me, 'You're never here when I need you.' But I have to perform in order to support Les Milandes. I can't be in two places at one time."

10

Joséphine and Jo Split

IN THE FALL OF 1956, JOSÉPHINE LEFT to perform in North Africa, where she had suffered through her serious illness during World War II. Those memories faded as she faced the new reality of the Algerian War. In a severe air-raid strike in a town called Palestro, almost the entire population had been massacred. The only survivors were two babies, a boy and a girl, found hidden underneath some rubble. They were taken to a hospital, where doctors determined that the two were not related. Joséphine adopted both children. She named the girl Marianne and decided she would be Catholic. She called the boy Brahim and determined his religion would be Muslim.

When Joséphine arrived at Les Milandes with the two new babies, Jo was furious. He scolded her about adding more children to their already sizeable family. The fact that one of the new children was a girl was especially upsetting to him. He reminded his wife that their children had no blood relationship and that adding a daughter to their collection of sons was asking for trouble. He also warned her she was spending money faster than they could earn it.

In 1957, Joséphine returned to the Ivory Coast, where she visited a hospital. When she discovered a young infant whose mother had died and whose father was unknown, she ignored her husband's warnings and adopted him. Koffi became the ninth member of the Rainbow Tribe. Joséphine's return with this child caused an argument so fierce that she ordered Jo to leave Les Milandes. He went to stay with friends in Paris, but he sent several people to talk to his wife to convince her to reconcile with him. She refused to consider it. She would not tolerate anyone telling her what to do.

A despondent Jo decided to take up his musical career again so that he could assure the financial future of their children. He did not want to divorce Joséphine, especially once he realized the devastating emotional effect that it could have on children already once separated from their parents. Newspapers reported the marital split in headlines like this one: THE HEART-RENDING DRAMA OF JOE AND JO, THOSE 50-YEAR-OLDS WITH BIG HEARTS. When Joséphine's friend Miki Sawada, who had helped her get the first child for the Rainbow Tribe, heard about the couple's separation, she wrote a letter begging them to reconcile. In her plea, she reminded the couple: "Having lost their natural parents, it would be unbearably cruel to be deprived of a mother and father again." The letter impressed Joséphine, and she told Jo about it, but she was still determined to be her own boss.

With her husband gone, Joséphine tried to manage the estate and care for the children, who lived in a converted stable block more like a boarding school dormitory than a home. Her temperamental nature could not tolerate the stress of so many responsibilities. She confused the children and upset their previously strict routines with her changeable nature. She did not discipline them because she wanted them to like her. If one of them misbehaved, she got a nurse or a nanny to apply the punishment. Joséphine showered the children with so many presents that they nicknamed her *Maman Cadeau*, or Mother Gift. Then she would leave them again to go perform. It was all or nothing in her relationship with the children, whose lives were most stable when she was gone.

Still, years later, the youngest, Stellina, who was probably the closest to Joséphine, said, "I was lucky. I think I had a wonderful mother. I never tried to judge her. I had ten years with her, after she died, ten years with my father in Argentina, but for me he was a stranger." However, while Joséphine toured and was separated from the children, Jo kept in contact with them, inviting them a few at a time to visit him in Paris.

In January 1959, Joséphine was en route from Rome to Istanbul when she received word of the sudden death of her mother, Carrie, at age 73. Joséphine accepted the news philosophically, believing death was a part of life, and did not return home to attend the funeral.

In that same year, while in Caracas, Venezuela, Joséphine adopted another boy. Mara's golden skin and coal-black eyes accented his native Venezuelan heritage, but like all the children in his desperately poor tribe, his legs were as thin as matchsticks and his belly was distended from malnutrition. Joséphine added: "Mara has rickets and a swollen stomach. When given food, he trembles and snatches . . . His mother worked out as a cook and left him alone on the ground all day with a piece of banana and coconut shell as his only toys." Maracaibo, the tribe's chief, had heard about Joséphine's Rainbow Tribe, and he decided to entrust his young grandson into her keeping. Because she was still on tour, Joséphine hired a nurse to take Mara home.

While Joséphine traveled and Jo remained in Paris, there was no one to supervise workers at the château. The situation was even worse when she was home because she treated the employees poorly, often criticizing one of them in front of others. But Joséphine had more serious problems than staff relations with which to contend. Because of the need to provide for her additional children, she needed more income. She agreed to return to the stage in Paris at the Olympia Theatre, where she had retired a few years earlier. In her usual style, Joséphine tackled rehearsals for *Paris Mes Amours*, or *Paris My Love*, with enthusiasm, but she expected everyone to conform to her workaholic schedule. She thought nothing of insisting the cast work until after midnight.

In December, a ragpicker was combing through the garbage in Paris when he found an infant boy. Joséphine heard about the child and rushed to claim it at the hospital where the baby had been taken. Although nurses had already given him the name André, Joséphine changed it to Noël because of the season when he was born.

Paris Mes Amours opened in May 1959 with Joséphine presenting several new tunes to audiences. One reviewer had mixed reactions: "Banking on the theory that Joséphine is a show in herself, Brunno Coquatrix hasn't provided much of a supporting show. . . . [Baker] neglects to sing any of her old songs—not even her theme, (J'ai deux amours.) In truth, her new material is only so-so. Press and public are so ecstatic at seeing Josie again that the flaws of (*Paris Mes Amours*) have escaped with scant mention. The Olympia has a hit that will run the summer and deep into next season." During one especially popular song, "Don't Touch Me Tomatoes," she dressed in a full-skirted, flouncy, West Indian costume and tossed fruits and vegetables to the audiences as she sang. She always closed with "Dans Mon Village," the song about her children.

Critics praised her performances, citing her development of a richer and truer voice. Joséphine and Jo remained on friendly terms, and his orchestra even played for several of her record-ings. As they worked together, they decided to try to work out their marital problems because, as Joséphine said, "We feel it is our duty to overcome all obstacles for the sake of our chil-dren." Jo moved back to Les Milandes. Despite their attempt to reconcile, the couple could not save their marriage. Joséphine explained to a reporter: "'We are not angry, but I have asked for a divorce on the grounds of incompatibility. Up to now, we have had very little time together; and until I left the stage, I have worked hard to do two things successfully' . . . to give a home

Joséphine and Jo pose with the first seven boys they adopted into the Rainbow Tribe. © Hulton-Deutsch Collection/CORBIS

to, and rear together, the nine children of different races she has adopted; and . . . to make Dordogne a progressive town . . . 'But Jo . . . does not agree with me in my two aims in life.'" They gave up on the marriage in 1962, and Jo moved to Argentina, where he opened a French restaurant.

In that same year, Joséphine adopted her final child. Her only daughter, Marianne, kept asking for a sister, since she felt isolated among the 10 boys. The second girl Joséphine chose to adopt was born in France to a Moroccan mother. Joséphine named the child Stellina. Despite the couple's separation, Jo signed the adoption papers, bringing the total children in the Rainbow Tribe to 12.

Over the next several years, the family's financial problems escalated. As Joséphine said in a newspaper interview, "I didn't realize when I retired that children cost so much money." From 1953 to 1963, Joséphine had lost $1.5 million and accumulated $400,000 in debt. To save Les Milandes, she once again had to pawn her jewelry, including the diamond-studded choker she had years ago bought for her cheetah Chiquita. By June 1963, her creditors were trying to force the sale of the château and its contents. Despite her money woes, Joséphine decided to expand the scope of her brotherhood movement. Instead of housing just the children in her Rainbow Tribe, she wanted Les Milandes to become an international College of Brotherhood. In August, she had the opportunity to earn some money for this latest project: a black American producer, Jack Jordan, invited her to appear at the 1963 March on Washington to promote civil rights and economic opportunity for blacks.

Joséphine agreed to attend the march, but she had trouble getting a visa. American officials refused to let her enter the country because of her actions and words years before in

MARCH ON WASHINGTON

On August 28, 1963, 250,000 people of all types—black and white, rich and poor, young and old, Hollywood stars and everyday people—gathered in Washington, DC, for a peaceful march to promote civil rights and job opportunities for black Americans. Participants walked down Constitution and Independence Avenues to the Lincoln Memorial, where they heard speeches, songs, and prayers by clergymen, civil rights leaders, politicians, and entertainers. The high point of the day was the Rev. Martin Luther King Jr.'s "I Have a Dream" speech.

Money for the march's organization came from the sale of buttons at 25 cents apiece, and from thousands of people who sent in small cash donations. Every detail was important because the planners believed that unless the march was peaceful and well organized, it would harm their cause. President Kennedy had even pre-signed executive orders to allow military intervention in case of rioting. But the march was a success and represented the belief that people of all races could work together for racial equality.

Argentina. She appealed to Attorney General Robert Kennedy, who overruled the objections and issued her a visa. He sent her a telegram regarding his decision that stated, "I am happy to inform you that your request for a visa has been granted and you will have it on Monday." He also told her that the delay had nothing to do with Cuba or civil rights but that she had not filled out the forms properly.

With visa in hand and wearing her French Air Auxiliary uniform with all of her medals, Joséphine joined the people who marched in the biggest civil rights demonstration in American history. She was among the seated guests on the platform and gave a brief two-and-a-half-minute speech, telling the audience: "You are here on the eve of a complete victory. You can't go wrong. The world is behind you. I've been following this movement for thirty years. Now that the fruit is ripe I want to be here. You can't put liberty at the top of the lips and expect people not to drink it. This is the happiest day of my life." She had made a similarly effusive comment when she performed before her first mixed-race audience in the United States.

Following the march, Joséphine was invited to appear in four benefit concerts at Carnegie Hall. The proceeds were to be divided among four civil rights charities and the Rainbow Tribe. Although Jordan had found backers to put up $15,000 for the concerts, he had difficulty finding a public relations person to manage Joséphine's performances. Many still remembered her anti-American statements in Argentina. Others had heard the stories about her failure to pay those who worked for her.

Finally, friends at the NAACP, one of the concerts' beneficiaries, persuaded Henri Ghent, a retired concert singer who wrote promotional materials for Columbia Records, to manage Joséphine. The youngest of 11 black children from a poor farm

CARNEGIE HALL

Beginning on May 30, 1890, Carnegie Hall was constructed over a period of seven years so New York citizens could enjoy music in a suitable concert hall. Andrew Carnegie, one of the world's richest men at the time, donated money to the city to build the music hall, and it was later named for him. Carnegie Hall was built as three connected buildings, with the main hall being the place where the music was performed. Over the years as various renovations occurred, this initial configuration presented some problems. The issues began when workers removed the roof, added a studio floor, and constructed a 10-story tower on the second building; this extra construction made Carnegie Hall difficult to navigate.

The first official performer in the hall was the famous composer Pyotr (Peter) Tchaikovsky. Since that first concert, most of the world's greatest performers and orchestras have appeared there. Ownership changed periodically, beginning with Mrs. Carnegie's sale to a realtor in 1925, six years after her husband's death. In March 1960, the hall was headed for demolition because of the need for massive renovations. At the last minute, interested parties stopped its destruction, and three months later New York City purchased the hall for five million dollars. It is now overseen by a nonprofit committee. Noted for its impeccable acoustics and Italian Renaissance–style architecture, the solidly built Carnegie Hall continues to be the site of spectacular musical performances with more than 180 concerts presented there every year.

in Georgia, Henri had followed a similar career path to that of Joséphine. Having heard all the stories about the difficulties of working with her, Henri nervously went to meet her at her suite in the New York Hilton. He was shocked to find an almost-bald woman, clad only in a flannel nightshirt that came to her knees, with her legs wrapped in pink elastic bandages to protect her joints from the cold. Instead of the difficult prima donna he expected, he found an almost childlike person who wanted desperately for American audiences to like her.

Using makeup tricks learned over the years, Joséphine managed to cover up the ravages of age while she was onstage. A wig covered her baldness caused by using congolene to straighten her hair. To camouflage the bags under her eyes, she dusted glitter under them and also added glitter across the bridge of her nose and on her lips. Wearing clothes that emphasized her small waist, her bust, and her hips, she appeared onstage in all her glamor, and the Carnegie Hall concerts were a success. Joséphine was still in the United States on November 22, 1963, when President John F. Kennedy was assassinated. In a six-word telegram, she communicated her shock and dismay to Jo in Argentina: "Our World is toppling. Affectionately yours."

In the meantime, the state of Les Milandes had begun to decline. Her employees frequently stole from the estate when Joséphine did not pay their wages. Because of her flamboyant lifestyle, merchants assumed she was wealthy and doubled the prices when they learned their products were going to the château. At that time, while Joséphine was staying in the Hotel Scribe in Paris, she met Jean-Claude Rouzaud, a 14-year-old porter who helped guests with their luggage and ran errands for them. The handsome, dark-haired teen came from a poor background where he and his family depended on friends to support them. After his father deserted the family, the teen had come to Paris to find work. He met Joséphine one day when he was asked to run an errand for her, and she sensed his loneliness. After they talked a while and she learned his story, Joséphine told him, "Don't be worried, my little one, you have no father, but from today on, you will have two mothers." She later unofficially adopted the boy and took him with her to Les Milandes. When he became a young adult, he took the last name Baker.

Creditors still hounded Joséphine to sell the property and pay all her debts. She ignored them and went back to Paris to appear in another show. In June the situation had become so critical that all of the utilities were turned off. In desperation, Joséphine invited some previous donors, bankers, and old friends to Les Milandes to discuss her finances. As a result, the popular French actress Brigitte Bardot went on television in 1964 to make an appeal for donations to save Les Milandes from its creditors. She spoke for only two and a half minutes, but donations poured in from all over the world. Although many people rescued her, not everyone thought Joséphine deserved charity, and several European newspapers ran criticisms. In Denmark, a man wrote a letter to the editor: "I, too, need $400,000. I don't have a castle or jewels or umpteen kids, but I need it because I'm broke. Is it necessary to live in a castle? Why doesn't Miss Baker just sell the whole thing and live in a decent house and bring up her kids like we all do?"

Following advice from others in the entertainment business, Joséphine set aside the donated money to care for the children. Although grateful for the assistance, she realized she would need 20 times more than she had to save the château and keep her children properly cared for. Joséphine continued to perform, keeping up a hectic pace as she had done years earlier, when she was much younger. On July 25, 1964, at age 58, she had a heart attack—the first of several she would suffer through over the next few years. Following her two-month hospitalization in Paris, a weakened Joséphine returned to Les Milandes. Unable to manage the children, she boarded them at a lycée, a French school for older children located about 12 miles from Les Milandes.

After a few weeks of rest, Joséphine resumed her grueling schedule—performances wherever she could schedule them, and appeals at conferences to gain support for the College of Brotherhood, which she still hoped to establish. She also spoke to the press about her aspirations for the college: "These youngsters will come here to learn how to live together. . . . We'll have a series of professors from different countries, of all colors and religions and all standards of life to teach the essentials of brotherhood." Creditors hovered over Les Milandes, waiting to confiscate it. The children, now all in their teens, took advantage of their mother's absences and lack of discipline when she was home. They became wild, displaying bad manners and a lack of respect for anyone but themselves. Joséphine's sister Margaret, who for many years had helped care for the children, was their most severe critic. She called them liars, cheaters, and spongers and even accused one of them of having stolen money she had saved for her own daughter's medicine. Harry Janes and his wife, an English couple who often cared for the children in the summer, were shocked at the children's irreverence and bad manners. Despite their atrocious behavior to others, the kids remained loyal to one another.

Joséphine herself admitted, "The older children are beginning to worry me." When she heard her first adopted child named Jean-Claude telling Moïse that he was superior because he was white, Joséphine couldn't believe that a member of her

Rainbow Tribe was racist. For just a little while, she wondered whether or not her plan to bring these adopted children together in a show of universal brotherhood had been a good idea.

11

Losing Les Milandes

By early November 1965, the creditors had become so insistent on repayment that Joséphine went to Morocco to beg King Hassan II for aid. In previous travels to that country, she became good friends with a woman named Kenza, who had close ties to the king. Joséphine relied on that relationship to persuade the king to help her financially. The monarch responded generously, giving her a $6,000 check, large enough to delay foreclosure on Les Milandes. He also promised her an annual donation of $20,000 to care for the children.

In July 1966, Fidel Castro invited Joséphine and her children to Cuba to celebrate the seventh anniversary of his revolution. He offered to pay all the family's expenses. Joséphine accepted the invitation, and she and the children enjoyed a peaceful vacation in a villa by the sea, about two miles from Havana. Joséphine gave a speech and sang for workers in the sugarcane fields. After leaving Cuba, Joséphine and the children went to Buenos Aires to see Jo. They had such a good visit that he agreed to come to the château for Christmas. Despite the restful trip, Joséphine became ill almost as soon as she arrived back in France. She had a recurrence of her intestinal problems from many years before and had to undergo a five-hour operation. The hospitalization costs added to her financial woes, and she decided to ask Castro for help since he had been so generous while she was in Cuba. He replied immediately that he was going to send her a present, which Joséphine interpreted as a pledge to provide financial assistance. Each day Joséphine anxiously awaited the mail's arrival. When Castro's present finally arrived, she was shocked to discover it was merely a box of two dozen oranges and six grapefruit.

Joséphine could have saved the château and solved many of her financial problems by selling some of the property, but she refused because she continued to dream of putting an international College of Brotherhood there. Still ignoring her financial straits, in 1967 Joséphine invited a team of Danish architects to visit Les Milandes for a month to develop a master plan for the design of such a college. They created a detailed proposal, for which Joséphine managed to avoid paying them. However, her creditors could be put off only so long, and 1968 brought about their demands for the sale of Les Milandes. The Olympia Theatre's director, Bruno Coquatrix, intervened on her behalf and got the sale annulled. Then he allowed her to perform at his theater to earn money to pay off her creditors. On June 6, after a short time there, she learned of the assassination of Attorney General Robert Kennedy. She left the show to fly to the United States so she could attend his funeral services at St. Patrick's Cathedral in New York City.

Joséphine took her five oldest sons with her to the funeral. For each of them she purchased a navy blazer, gray flannel slacks, and black shoes. During the entire flight Joséphine embroidered tiny red-, white-, and blue-striped flags and the word FRANCE on each of the blazers. When he heard about the travel, Coquatrix was dismayed that she had bought six round-trip tickets that cost more than she had earned performing in his show. Worse still, Joséphine had a mild stroke upon her return to France. Her creditors backed off for a short while, but on September 22, 1968, she was served with an eviction notice.

France had a law that a family with children could not be evicted during cold weather, so she actually had until March 15 to remove herself and her family from the premises. Her sister Margaret still owned a house in the village that had sprung up around Les Milandes, and Joséphine and her children could have gone there to live. But Joséphine would not even consider this option, and in early 1969, she quietly left Les Milandes and moved to Paris to stay with her younger children in a cramped two-bedroom apartment provided by Marie Spiers, the wife of Joséphine's musical accompanist.

Moïse explained what it was like for him and the other children to leave their home for the last time:

> When we left Les Milandes at the end of the school vacation, we were convinced that we would never see our château again. Still, in our heart of hearts, we hoped for a miracle. That came from living with *Maman*. We'd seen her move mountains so often. . . . "Not this time," Akio insisted. He knew best. After all, he was the oldest, the boss, the one *Maman* left in charge in her absence. Jean-Claude, Brahim, Mara and I, the family "tough guys," decided to knock down the cabin we had built in the woods. If we couldn't enjoy it, no one would! Armed with pickaxes from the toolshed, we set to work angrily. As the cabin fell to bits, so did our childhood.

With the château empty, Joséphine's creditors moved in and began to auction off her personal and household goods.

Joséphine's personal objects put up for sale at the auction of household items to help pay her debts. © *Pierre Vauthey/Sygma/ Corbis*

French film actor Jean-Claude Brialy, who had recently purchased a restaurant in Paris, invited Joséphine to perform in his
cabaret beginning on March 27, 1969. She agreed, but before
the opening, the purchasers of Les Milandes claimed they were
moving into the château prior to March 15. In Joséphine's eyes,
the property was hers until that date. She left the children in
Paris with Marie Spiers and returned to the château, where she
barricaded herself in the kitchen. She notified reporters and
photographers about what she was doing and posed for pictures
while giving numerous interviews about her plight. She first told
them, "I will not leave." And then later to a reporter for *Le Figaro*,
she said, "I'm not bitter. We can all live in a tent." Fewer than 40
years before, Joséphine had been named the richest black woman
in the world. Now she was destitute and effectively homeless.

The new owners of Les Milandes were tired of her dramatics,
and on March 12 at 7:00 AM, eight brawny men forced their way
into the house. They grabbed Joséphine by her head, arms, and
legs and roughly carried her outside. It was raining, and they
dumped her on the wet ground. She was still in her nightgown
and had a plastic shower cap over her bald head. With a blanket
wrapped around her knees and holding a kitten, she sat shivering on the château's front steps for seven hours. Eventually
Henriette Malaury, a neighbor, took pity on her and contacted a
judge who ruled that Joséphine could stay in the château three
more days. But by then Joséphine had already fallen ill. She col-
lapsed on the steps, and an ambulance took her to a hospital in
Perigueux, a nearby village.

While in the hospital, she scribbled her final thoughts about
Les Milandes on a tablet:

It was here that my Rainbow Tribe got its start. I hope
that in years to come my children will represent every

point of view as well as all colors and religions, because that is where true freedom lies. My young ones haven't let me down. They are genuine brothers and sisters who deeply love one another. *The Rainbow Tribe has advanced us all a thousand years.*

With her usual resilience, Joséphine regained her strength quickly. Just two weeks after collapsing, she was performing at the Paris cabaret, where owner Jean-Claude Brialy served as her master of ceremonies. He referred to the cabaret as Chez Joséphine for as long as she performed there. On opening night, a large group of famous performers—including Italian actress Sophia Loren, Princess Grace of Monaco, British musician Mick Jagger, and French actor and businessman Alain Delon—attended to show their support for Joséphine; many of them she barely knew. She gave 57 performances, one every night of the week except Mondays when the restaurant was closed.

In June, while the children were not in school, Joséphine took them to Spain to vacation with some friends. Then in late July, she traveled to Monaco to give a benefit performance for the country's Red Cross, of which Grace Kelly was president. Princess Grace had been in the Stork Club the night Joséphine was denied service and admired Joséphine's spirit in standing up to the club owner and later to Walter Winchell. She said, "I wonder if I could have done the same." Over the years Princess Grace had followed Joséphine's activities and was familiar with her Rainbow Tribe, her desire for a College of Brotherhood, and her battle to hold on to Les Milandes.

During the rehearsal for the benefit, the two women met, and Princess Grace discovered that Joséphine and her children were in effect homeless.

GRACE KELLY

Born in Philadelphia in 1929, Grace Kelly decided at an early age to become an actress. After finishing high school, she went to New York to enroll in the American Academy of Dramatic Arts. When she was unsuccessful in getting acting roles on Broadway after graduation, she became a model for magazines like *Cosmopolitan* and *Redbook*. The film industry boomed after World War II, and Grace soon found success acting in movies. She starred in 11 films and over 60 television productions. She played opposite many of the famous male actors of the day, and in 1954 she received the Academy Award for Best Actress for her role in *The Country Girl*.

While at the Cannes Film Festival in Paris in 1950, she met Prince Rainier Grimaldi III of Monaco, who was searching for a bride. The cool sophistication of the beautiful blonde appealed to him, and he decided to ask Grace to become his wife. After the two married, she became Princess Grace of Monaco. Her husband insisted she give up her acting career and even banned her films in Monaco. The couple had three children: Caroline, Albert, and Stéphanie. In 1982, Grace was driving her Rover with her youngest daughter, Stéphanie, as a passenger. Grace suffered a mini-stroke, causing her to lose control of the car, which plunged down a cliff. After 24 hours in a coma, the princess died at the age of 52.

The princess arranged for the Monacan Red Cross to give Joséphine a $20,000 down payment on a $100,000 villa in Roquebrune-Cap-Martin, a coastal town about three miles from Monte Carlo. She also arranged for a guaranteed mortgage so Joséphine would never have to worry about being evicted. From the villa that Joséphine named Villa Maryvonne, she could see the Grimaldi castle where Grace and Prince Rainier lived. In September the children came from Spain to join their mother in their new home. Joséphine's sister Margaret moved nearby so that she could help care for the Rainbow Tribe.

Joséphine easily fit into the simple, quiet lifestyle of Roquebrune-Cap-Martin, where she made no effort to have people recognize her. However, sad feelings often overwhelmed her, because as the children grew older, they drew further away from her. The 10 sons, only seven years apart in age, became wild and unruly teenagers. Growing up under the care of nannies and nurses, the children had bonded with one another, not with their parents. Now in young adulthood, their relationship to Joséphine was not a close one. Her disapproval of their drinking, wearing hippie-style clothing, and staying out most of the night had no effect on them. Sometimes she blamed the situation on their not having had a father and felt guilty about having driven Jo away.

Unfortunately she could not remedy the situation since she had little time to remain at home and nurture closer ties to her children. She still had to earn a living to support all of them, and doing so became more difficult with each passing year. In her mid-60s, Joséphine no longer received invitations to be in the large, glamorous shows. Rather, she performed mostly at clubs, hotels, or charitable events.

In 1970, Joséphine again appeared at the annual Red Cross Gala in Monte Carlo. Even though she was no longer a big star, she had not been forgotten. A distinguished committee wanted to lobby for her to receive the Nobel Peace Prize. She refused the idea, saying, "I don't deserve this great honour. It should be shared by each man and woman on this earth who struggles to love and live in peace with his neighbor and himself. We're all created in God's image and we're all each other's redemption, resurrection and miracle. I believe in redemption. I believe in resurrection. I believe in miracles."

Even as her other children withdrew from her, her 13th child, 27-year-old Jean-Claude Rouzaud, grew closer to Joséphine and helped to find her jobs performing. When he visited her at Maryvonne, he acted as an older brother to the other children and sat at the head of the table at meals. His unofficial role as caretaker in the family was not well received by the rest of the Rainbow Tribe, many of whom considered him an outsider. One time, after some rebellion by the children, Joséphine surprised them by announcing that the second Jean-Claude would read a letter from her doctor. "Dear Boys and Girls," read Jean-Claude, "You are being very mean to your mother. You are killing her. If you don't start being nice soon, she will die." As he concluded, Joséphine stood for a minute, almost as though she were going to bow, and then ran to her bedroom. The letter and her actions frightened the younger children, and the youngest, Stellina, started to cry. One of the older boys scoffed, "Don't be silly. It's an act. She's nutty. Leave her alone."

However, Jean-Claude recognized how much Joséphine yearned to be a good mother to the Rainbow Tribe. He explained, "For fun, she would take all of us out to a restaurant together to eat and dance. Of course, it was always at the expense of someone else, but it was fabulous. Mostly she liked to go for walks, or to an amusement park or the theatre. Her favorite outing was the zoo. She loved to see the animals through the eyes of the children."

In 1972, Joséphine received a welcome invitation: the American promoter Jack Jordan— who had arranged for her to appear at Carnegie Hall after the civil rights march on Washington— asked her to perform there again. This time proceeds from the four performances would benefit the United Nations Children's Fund, otherwise known as UNICEF.

UNICEF

The United Nations Children's Fund (UNICEF) was founded in 1946 to provide food, clothing, and health care to European children suffering from famine and disease after World War II. It became a permanent part of the United Nations seven years later, and it is now active in 190 countries and territories. UNICEF's goal is to give children the best start in life so that they can have a bright future. It promotes education for girls, immunizations against common childhood diseases, and sufficient nourishment to grow strong, healthy bodies. UNICEF also works to prevent the spread of HIV/AIDS among young people.

In times of dire emergency, UNICEF is present to relieve suffering and to prevent exploitation. According to its mission statement, the organization is committed to ensuring special protection for the most disadvantaged children—victims of war, disasters, extreme poverty, disease, and those with disabilitie—so that they will have a world in which the rights of all children are recognized.

The shows would also be a celebration of the 50 years since Joséphine first appeared in the road company of *Shuffle Along*. At first she was reluctant to go to America again. She protested, "Nobody wants me. They've forgotten me." But Jordan and her sister Margaret convinced Joséphine that she should give it a try, and plans were made for her to travel to the United States in 1973. Before she left, Marshal Tito, president of Yugoslavia, invited Joséphine to visit him and his wife to talk about the possibility of helping her establish the College of Brotherhood. Although Tito offered to let her use a small castle for her school, Joséphine realized she no longer had the energy to pursue such an involved endeavor. Nothing else ever came of the idea.

As soon as she returned from her visit with Tito, it was time for Joséphine to head to the United States for her performances at Carnegie Hall, where her longtime friend, 80-year-old Bricktop, would introduce her. Joséphine's return to the New York stage was marked by glittering, exaggerated costumes. On opening night, her 67th birthday, she appeared in a net body stocking that sparkled with beads and sequins. She wore a four-foot-high headdress made of orange feathers, and in her hand she held a rhinestone-studded microphone. For other performances she wore similar extravagant outfits. The show itself was a mixture of old and new songs, both of which were well received by New York audiences. For the four performances she earned $120,000, temporarily removing the specter of poverty.

After the time at Carnegie Hall, Joséphine wanted to return to Monaco, but Jack Jordan had arranged a two-month tour for her in the United States. Showing some of the stubborn spirit from her younger days, Joséphine told him: "I don't understand what you are talking about because my English isn't very good. But you know something? I listen when I hear the money. And it doesn't sound like the right money . . . you keep on talking and when you get finished you let me know what the outcome is. *Goooood night!"*

With that challenge she went home to Monaco, only to find a new problem. Her older daughter Marianne, who was just entering her teens, had run away. Although she eventually returned, during the heartbreaking time she was gone, Joséphine developed severe irregular heartbeats. She was admitted to the American Hospital in Paris, where her heart was stopped and restarted to restore the rhythm. Doctors recommended that she have complete rest for at least four months and then a quieter lifestyle for a year. Joséphine could not obey their orders. She still had to earn a living to support herself and the children, and she insisted on meeting a contract obligation in Copenhagen, Denmark. She feared that if the public learned how ill she had been, she would get no more performance offers. Only a week out of the hospital, she was working her usual 12-hour days.

By September 1973, Jordan had amassed enough money to attract Joséphine back to the United States for the 17-city tour he had arranged. Jean-Claude accompanied her on the tour and began to use Baker as his last name. When Joséphine had a four-day break in the schedule, she accepted an invitation from Prime Minister Golda Meir to fly to Israel to celebrate the country's 25 years of existence. Joséphine was one of only 450 invited guests. She attended the official activities, but she also visited in the home of an Arab porter she met at the Jerusalem International Hotel, where she was staying. He lived in the West Bank village of Bethany. At his home, she noticed the family used a block of ice to chill their food. When Joséphine returned to Jerusalem, she sent an electric refrigerator to his home. This was a generous act that she could not afford.

Because she took time to make arrangements about the refrigerator, Joséphine was a day late returning from Israel to her next performance in San Francisco. Jordan had to refund money to the sold-out crowd, and he lost thousands of dollars. He told Joséphine that he planned to take the lost money out of her pay. She responded by quitting the show. She had Jean-Claude pack up all her costumes and she returned home to France.

By this time, Jean-Claude was becoming tired of Joséphine's unpredictable nature. He didn't want to leave the United States, where he had hoped to stay and get work. To gain attention for himself, he talked freely to members of the press about Joséphine. One newspaperman claimed Jean-Claude announced Joséphine's engagement to a Mexican artist, Robert Brady. Although Jean-Claude denied having done so, Joséphine threw a temper tantrum. Back in France, she dumped him. Jean-Claude was shocked: "I saw her use everybody, but I never thought she would do it to me. I said to myself: 'But I am her son!' It made no difference."

Joséphine returned to New York for a weeklong Christmas show at the Palace Theatre on Broadway, an arrangement made by Jean-Claude before their split. The Palace was the most impressive vaudeville theater in America at that time. However, when she arrived, she did not receive the usual welcome for a star. Instead of her name being in large letters on the 10-story-high billboard, her name appeared only in small aluminum letters on the marquee. In addition, Jordan hired a group of picketers to march outside the theater to protest Joséphine's having broken her contract with him.

Even worse, no efforts had been made inside the theater to even clean the stage, and the band seemed bored by her performance. Despite Joséphine's hard work during rehearsals, opening night did not go well. Advancing age and poor health dimmed her memory, and she sometimes forgot the words to the songs as she sang. Despite a negative preshow review and a bad rehearsal, when the show opened, Joséphine sang 12 songs and made the accompanying costume changes, gave monologues, and danced the Charleston. At the end, the audience rose as one to give her a standing ovation that lasted 30 minutes.

Joséphine went through a remarkable transformation when she performed. People who saw her in the dressing room before the show could not believe the change that took place in front of their eyes. She seemed 20 years younger in the spotlight than she did in daylight. Thanks to makeup and stage lighting, the bags under her eyes disappeared. Her spine straightened and her thighs tightened. Her chin lifted and her head went back. When she received the cue to go onstage, the fading 64-year-old woman became a glamorous star filled with energy.

12

The Curtain Falls

WITH JEAN-CLAUDE NO LONGER at her beck and call, Joséphine took her nephew Richard Jr. with her as she made the rounds of galas and receptions in New York. Even after her many years of financial woes, she treated 20 people to a steak and champagne dinner at the Waldorf Astoria Hotel. The extravagant expense shocked Richard, and he asked her how she planned to pay for it. Her response was typical Joséphine: "I have an image to maintain and I'm going to maintain it."

The expensive dinner caught the attention of a private New York club called Raffles, whose clientele were wealthy and well known. The small club hired Joséphine to perform during January and February 1974. Opening night brought out such celebrities as actresses Debbie Reynolds and Paulette Goddard, and artist Andy Warhol. Despite the glittering crowd, Joséphine was too tired to put on a good show. Yet for some reason, reviewers were kind about her poor performances, and she received invitations to several other nightspots. By April she was exhausted from performing so many shows, and she returned to Monaco.

Meanwhile, Jean-Claude had realized that Joséphine's dropping him was the best thing that could have happened to his career. Using money saved from the sale of a nightclub he had owned in West Berlin, he went back to New York, where he kept the last name Baker and produced a French-language cable TV show that included documentaries, news programs, and dramas shown internationally. On West 42nd Street, he also opened a restaurant that he called Chez Joséphine.

Back at Maryvonne in Monaco, Joséphine continued to be plagued by money worries. She owed social security payments for her employees, and taxes to more than one government. She had huge telephone bills of as much as $800 a week; many of the calls were international. While she was gone, her children charged untold amounts at the local shops. Joséphine paid each of her creditors a little bit at a time, hoping to keep them happy until she could pay the bills in full. Because of her failing memory, she had the additional expense of having to hire a secretary named Marie-Joli to help with correspondence. Marie-Joli arrived for work on the first day driving a white Fiat. Joséphine took one look at it and decided she wanted such a car for herself. The secretary's first correspondence for Joséphine was a letter to Gianni Agnelli, president of Fiat in Italy, asking him to give her a Fiat. He did.

Just as she almost despaired of ever being free of financial worries, André Levasseur, her costume designer for the past 10 years, proposed putting on a special celebration for that year's Monacan Red Cross Gala. It would be a review celebrating Joséphine's 50 years in French show business. Her former employer, cabaret owner Jean-Claude Brialy, agreed to be the master of ceremonies for *Joséphine*, which would tell her life story in song and dance. Although she would be onstage for most of the show, younger dancers would portray Joséphine as a young woman.

Joséphine onstage for the production of *Joséphine* with master of ceremonies, French actor Jean-Claude Brialy. © *René Maestri/ Sygma/Corbis*

Joséphine was excited about the show, especially since her children would see her in a performance that reflected her early glory days for the first time. The revue received such acclaim from reviewers and audiences alike that the producers decided to take it to Paris. Joséphine rejoiced at the thought of returning to the scene of her earliest show-business victories. However, the big theaters refused to book the performance because of her poor health. The director at the Casino de Paris, where she had triumphed in earlier years, offered to make an exception if Joséphine allowed a young, promising black dancer to practice alongside her and be prepared to take her place if Joséphine should become ill. Joséphine refused, adamantly stating, "Nobody can take my place."

Her refusal to have an understudy closed the door on any big theater possibilities, so the producers decided to use a former music hall called the Bobino Theatre.

Being in Paris again infused Joséphine with new energy as the show's rehearsals continued throughout early 1975. Even her memory seemed improved, but the producers took no chances and placed large cue cards on the floor all around the Bobino stage. Before the official opening, a TV news crew interviewed Joséphine and asked her if her children had seen the show. They were all at school, but she told the newsmen, "At this moment it is good they are not here, because when I'm with them, I forget everything. . . . Only my children count. And right now it is

BOBINO THEATRE

The Bobino Theatre was a small music hall in the neighborhood of Montparnasse on the left bank of the River Seine in Paris. For over 100 years, the city's best singers appeared there. Located on the Rue de la Gaité, which means "street of joy," it was surrounded by cafes, bars, and small restaurants. Its audiences were made up of students, workers, artists, and small-business people. To provide an appropriate setting for *Joséphine*, the owners extended the stage, put new carpet in the building, enlarged the orchestra pit, and provided more space for costume storage. The Bobino stopped functioning as a theater in 1983, after 183 years. Today it is a cabaret.

necessary that I have peace and tranquility so I can give myself entirely to the public of Paris."

The positive audience reaction to the show when it was performed in several small theaters convinced the producers that *Joséphine* was a hit, and they booked it weeks in advance. When the show opened on April 8, 1975, Joséphine appeared in costumes representing her lifetime of performances. The 34 songs she sang in 15 scenes also came from her life. She ended the show with "Paris Paname," a new song written especially for her. The audience loved her and gave her a 30-minute standing ovation.

One reviewer praised her comeback as an eternal return. A dinner at the Bristol for 250 people followed and honored her 50 years in show business. The table centerpiece was a seven-tiered cake iced with spun sugar that Princess Grace helped her cut. It was 4:00 AM when Joséphine finally left the Bristol and her admirers.

After the final curtain fell on Wednesday night, the second evening of the performance, Joséphine and several of her costars went to a restaurant across the street from the theater to eat her favorite meal, spaghetti. Next she wanted to go dancing, but the others pled weariness and went home. Joséphine, only two months away from her 69th birthday, replied, "Tired? Young people are no fun anymore."

Thursday, April 10, was a typical day—phone calls, a light lunch, and an afternoon nap. She had a 5:00 PM appointment with a journalist, so Pepito's niece Lélia Scotto, who was staying with Joséphine, went to wake her up for the appointment. Joséphine was sleeping so soundly that the young woman hesitated to disturb her. She waited a while and then decided that it was rude to keep the journalist waiting longer. Lélia tried to awaken Joséphine but could not because, about an hour earlier, Joséphine had drifted into a coma caused by a stroke.

Joséphine triumphantly appears before an audience in her final performance at the Bobino Theatre in Paris.
© *James Andanson/Sygma/Corbis*

The doctor who responded to Lélia's frantic call sent an ambulance to transport Joséphine to Pitié-Salpêtrière, a nearby hospital with the best emergency room in Paris.

Both Princess Grace and Joséphine's sister Margaret rushed to the hospital upon hearing that Joséphine had been taken there. Doctors said there was a 70 percent chance Joséphine would be impaired if they performed surgery. Margaret refused to let them operate, knowing her sister would never have been happy if she could not walk or talk. Joséphine died at the hospital the next day on Saturday, April 12, at about 5:00 in the morning. Princess Grace issued a statement to the press, assuring all who had loved Joséphine that the star's last years had been happy ones.

On the hotel bed where Lélia had been unable to rouse Joséphine was a pile of newspapers. Apparently Joséphine had been enjoying the enthusiastic reviews of her latest triumph. When she was 21, Joséphine had told Marcel Sauvage, one of her biographers: "I shall dance all my life. I was born to dance, just for that. To live is to dance. I would like to die breathless, spent, at the end of a dance." She accomplished that goal, and although her death certificate showed "cerebral hemorrhage" [a type of stroke that causes bleeding inside the brain] as the cause of death, many who knew her well believed she died of joy over her triumphant return to the Paris stage at the age of 69.

On April 15, 1975, at 12:00 PM, a procession stretched across the city, carrying Joséphine's body from the hospital to the Church of the Madeleine. It paused in front of the Bobino Theatre, where her name still blazed in lights. Gray, overcast skies added to the sober mood of the 20,000 mourners who turned out for the funeral. Only 3,000 attendees could fit inside the church; others amassed on the steps and spilled out onto the sidewalks of the square. The number of flashbulbs popping made it seem more like a theater opening than a funeral.

PITIÉ-SALPÊTRIÈRE HOSPITAL

Pitié-Salpêtrière Hospital, located near the Seine River in Paris, is one of Europe's largest teaching hospitals. However, it has a long and unusual history dating back to 1656 when King Louis XIV of France decided to rid Paris of some of the 50,000 beggars, homeless people, thieves, and prostitutes who roamed the streets each day. He ordered the design of a building to house these people. Construction began in 1620 on a site that previously housed a gunpowder factory. Since gunpowder's main ingredient is saltpeter (potassium nitrate), the name transferred to the hospital, La Salpêtrière.

The building was completed in 1680, and 5,000 of the city's poor—mostly women—were forced to stay in the hospital. In 1684, a women's prison and juvenile detention home were added. For many years after that, the facility served as more of a detention center than as a hospital. Eventually, the hospital had four sections: detention for juveniles whom the city hoped to rehabilitate, a place for prostitutes, a women's jail, and a large accommodation for women deemed insane.

Over time, the hospital developed a reputation for providing humane treatment of people with mental illness, and its researchers made great strides in the study of multiple sclerosis and Parkinson's disease. In 1964, La Salpêtrière merged with another hospital, La Pitié, and today is known as Pitié-Salpêtrière. With a capacity for over 2,000 patients, the hospital provides more than 70 services.

Since she was a decorated war hero, Joséphine received a full military funeral. Pallbearers carried the heavy black coffin up the aisle to the spot where Joséphine's military decorations rested on a purple pillow in front of the altar. The 24 flags of the French Army adorned the massive auditorium, and Jo and the children had placed a huge heart of red roses near the casket. After a few remarks by the priest, the family followed the coffin outside as a harpist played "J'ai Deux Amours" for the last time.

Princess Grace felt the Paris funeral had not been respectful enough with all of the media presence, so Joséphine's family agreed to hold a more somber one in Monaco after her body

Princess Grace attending the burial she had arranged for Joséphine Baker in the Monaco Cemetery. © René Maestri/Sygma/ Corbis

arrived there. The princess took charge of this ceremony, and the press was not allowed entry. The coffin lay inside the sanctuary, an honor usually reserved for royalty. Then it was moved to a mausoleum where it remained for six months until a space could be found for interment in the crowded Monacan cemetery.

Both fans and critics have pondered how Joséphine reached universal stardom as well as convinced so many people to come to her financial aid over and over again. She began as a poor little girl who escaped life in the slums of St. Louis to dance in some of the first black musicals performed in America. From there she traveled to France, where she won the hearts of Parisians with her spontaneous dancing and clowning around. She answered the call of her adopted country by serving in France's military during World War II. When the conflict ended, she sought out a man who could be a father to the Rainbow Tribe, 12 children she adopted, all from different ethnic, racial, and religious backgrounds. She continued her roles on the stage, traveling throughout Europe, to South America, and eventually back to the United States, where she joined in the civil rights movement. She became homeless only to be befriended by Princess Grace of Monaco and ended her career once again on the Paris stage, beloved by the thousands who flocked to see her.

Joséphine had admirers in the art and literary worlds as well as in her world of entertainment. Artists, including Pablo Picasso, clamored to paint her portrait. American author Ernest Hemingway called her "the most sensational woman anybody ever saw." With her fantastic appeal, she enchanted even heads of state. To each person in her audience she communicated the feeling that she was sitting on their lap, singing only for them.

She carried this stage charisma into her relationships outside the theater, making each person who ever aided her feel that he or she was the only one who had ever done so. Both her admirers and her benefactors had difficulty accepting that Joséphine was dead—that the star was extinguished.

Appendix

THE RAINBOW TRIBE

In 2006, for the 100th anniversary of Joséphine Baker's birth, the artist known as Chouski was selected to sculpt a statue of Joséphine to go in the park below Les Milandes, the childhood home of the Rainbow Tribe. The work of art was revealed on June 3, 2006, at a special ceremony where singers and a jazz orchestra played many of the songs for which Joséphine was famous.

The statue depicts Joséphine standing and hugging a little boy, most likely her first adopted son, Akio, to her chest. Joséphine looks peaceful in the representation of the dream she had pursued throughout her adult life—to prove that people of all nationalities, colors, and races could live together in harmony. The footprints of her 12 children are carved into the statue's pedestal.

Most of the Rainbow Tribe have lived quiet lives since reaching adulthood, and finding information about their current activities is difficult.

Akio, the first adopted child, turned 62 in July 2014. He is a short, mild-mannered man who is unmarried and works in a bank. He didn't speak until he was four years old and he remains a quiet person to this day. Once a year, he leaves his work in Paris to travel to Les Milandes, where he serves as a guide to tourists interested in his mother's clothing, costumes (especially the banana skirt), posters, and other memorabilia. He is the only member of the Rainbow Tribe who still returns to their childhood home.

Janot, who is also single, works as a gardener for the Société des Bains de Mer in Monte Carlo.

Luis is married to Michele; they have two children; he works for an insurance company in Monte Carlo and lives in Menton, France. Their first child was born and died shortly after Joséphine's death; the infant is buried beside her.

Jari now spells his name Jarry. He has not returned to the château in over two decades. At age eight, he was sent to live with his father because Joséphine discovered he was gay. He is short and blond with red cheeks. He is single, lives in New York, and works as a waiter at the Chez Josephine on 42nd Street. The restaurant acts as a constant reminder of his mother, whose pictures and photos adorn all the walls. He and Akio have the closest relationship of the 12 siblings.

The first Jean-Claude is single and is writing a collection of short stories. He lives in Paris.

Moïse is divorced and has no children. He currently lives in his birth country of Israel.

Brahim is also single, and just finished his first novel. He lives in Paris and has changed his name to Brian.

Marianne is married with two children; she lives in Paris. She gave birth to Joséphine's first grandchild, Marie-Audrey.

Koffi is married. He lives in Buenos Aires with his family and works as a chef de cuisine.

Mara is married with two children. He works in a government tax office in Benson, France.

Noël is single and lives in Paris.

Stellina is single. She works for an airline and she lives in Paris.

Though not part of the original Rainbow Tribe, Jean-Claude Baker became close to Joséphine in his adult years. He became an American citizen in 1983 and currently lives in New York City, where he operates Chez Josephine. When asked about the Rainbow Tribe, he always drily says that they are alive and that no one is in jail.

In 1991, on a French television show, 11 of the Rainbow Tribe were reunited for the first time since Joséphine's death. Only Noël, who was at the time hospitalized for schizophrenia, did not participate.

NOTES

1: Her Own Journey

"*I'm leaving here a nobody*": Remembering Josephine, 1976, page 33.

"*Mama said things to me*": The Josephine Baker Story, 2000, page 16.

"*No! No! Please don't*": Josephine, 1977, page 8.

"*I scream, I scream, Mother*": Josephine: The Hungry Heart, 1993, page 24.

"*Oh, it's the ghost*": Josephine: The Hungry Heart, 1993, page 25.

"*Never again would I*": Josephine, 1977, page 11.

"*I throw myself*": Josephine: The Hungry Heart, 1993, page 20.

"*I'm going to talk*": Josephine, 1977, page 14.

"*It worked! I'm hired!*": Josephine, 1977, page 14.

"*Margaret, before I say*": Josephine, 1977, page 16.

"*She has chosen her path*": Josephine: The Hungry Heart, 1993, page 40.

2: Show Business Debut

"Seeing everybody looking": Naked at the Feast, 1981, page 28.

"Many of us had been": Josephine: The Hungry Heart, 1993, pages 63–64.

"If somebody came": The Josephine Baker Story, 2000, page 44.

"I had grown used to": Josephine, 1977, page 31.

"I can sing all": Josephine, 1977, page 40.

"Paris is the most beautiful city": Josephine, 1977, page 42.

"I can only recall": Josephine: The Hungry Heart, 1993, page 97.

3: Joséphine Charms Paris

"You're fixin' t'kill": The Josephine Baker Story, 2000, page 73.

"Miz Dudley, why": The Josephine Baker Story, 2000, page 73.

"You must let me shape this show": The Josephine Baker Story, 2000, page 78.

"The first time I": Josephine: The Hungry Heart, 1993, page 6.

"This isn't New York": Josephine, 1977, page 52.

"Well, last night after": Josephine: The Hungry Heart, 1993, page 116.

"they are as simple": Josephine: The Hungry Heart, 1993, page 21.

"No one wanted to": Josephine: The Hungry Heart, 1993, page 118.

"As beautiful as the night": Josephine Baker, 1988, page 20.

"lamentable transatlantic": Naked at the Feast, 1981, page 64.

"I had plotted to": Josephine: The Hungry Heart, 1993, page 122.

"Don't count on it": Jazz Cleopatra, 1989, page 88.

"If you want me": Josephine: The Hungry Heart, 1993, page 129.

"I felt like kicking": Josephine: The Hungry Heart, 1993, page 129.

"I never recognized": Josephine: The Hungry Heart, 1993, page 131.

4: *La Folie du Jour*

"A hat went flying": *The Josephine Baker Story*, 2000, page 113.

"I don't have the calling": *Naked at the Feast*, 1981, page 97.

"I tell them everything": *Naked at the Feast*, 1981, page 103.

"tall, vital, incomparably": *The Josephine Baker Story*, 2000, page
108.

"After the show": *Josephine*, 1977, page 66.

"I got sparkling rings": *The Josephine Baker Story*, 2000, page 119.

"and the queens were": *Josephine: The Hungry Heart*, 1993,
page 13.

"I am tired of this": *Naked at the Feast*, 1981, page 128.

"I will marry an average": *Naked at the Feast*, 1981, page 128.

"I'm just as happy": *Naked at the Feast*, 1981, page 132.

"He sure is a count": "Josephine Baker, Black Dancer, Weds a
Real Count." *Milwaukee Journal*, June 22, 1977.

"I couldn't tell you. When I dance, I dance": *Josephine: The Hungry
Heart*, 1993, page 159.

"He wounded himself": *The Josephine Baker Story*, 2000,
page 148.

"I don't want to live": *The Josephine Baker Story*, 2000, pages
153–54.

5: Two Loves

"Joséphine had to have": *Naked at the Feast*, 1981, pages 174–75.

"The closest I can come to telling": *Josephine: The Hungry Heart*,
1993, page 164.

"The beautiful savage has learned to discipline": *Josephine: The Hungry Heart*, 1993, page 171.

"*She could be very bossy*": *Naked at the Feast*, 1981, page 177.

"*The sight of Josephine*": *Josephine: The Hungry Heart*, 1993, page 175.

"*I'm so excited*": *Naked at the Feast*, 1981, page 197.

6: Storms of Life

"*She just slept*": *Josephine: The Hungry Heart*, 1993, page 194.

"*My grandmother's apartment*": *Josephine: The Hungry Heart*, 1993, page 194.

"*After her cyclonic*": *The Josephine Baker Story*, 2000, page 197.

"*Critics aren't fooled*": *The Josephine Baker Story*, 2000, page 197.

"*Cheríe, I am not going to speak of love*": *Josephine*, 1977, page 110.

"*He is a great artist*": *The Josephine Baker Story*, 2000, page 217.

"*France made me*": *The Josephine Baker Story*, 2000, page 214.

"*We are informed*": *The Josephine Baker Story*, 2000, page 222.

"*I think that* monsieur": *The Josephine Baker Story*, 2000, page 222.

7: Joséphine's Challenges

"*Why don't you just put a zipper*": *Josephine: The Hungry Heart*, 1993, page 245.

"*as much a victim*": *Josephine: The Hungry Heart*, 1993, page 248.

"*Tumpy ain't dead.*" *Josephine: The Hungry Heart*, 1993, page 248.

"*That's the Americans*": *Naked at the Feast*, 1981, pages 229–30.

"*There has been a slight*": *Josephine: The Hungry Heart*, 1993, page 249.

"*We've got to show that blacks and whites*": *Josephine*, 1977, page 131.

"*My program included*": *Babylon Girls: Black Women Performers and the Shaping of the Modern*, 2009, page 260.

"Dear Mademoiselle Josephine Baker": *Naked at the Feast*, 1981, page 237.

8: Let My People Go

"under police guard": *Josephine: The Hungry Heart*, 1993, page 280.

"I do not like people": *Josephine Baker*, 1988, page 160.

"There is a fundamental": *Josephine*, 1977, page 161.

"This is the happiest moment of my life": *The Josephine Baker Story*, 2000, page 254.

"Josephine Baker's applause": *Naked at the Feast*, 1981, pages 248–49.

"They have killed": *Naked at the Feast*, 1981, page 250.

"This is a terrible experience": "Stork Club Refused to Serve Her, Josephine Baker Claims." *Milwaukee Journal*, October 19, 1951.

"I am appalled at the agony": *Jazz Cleopatra*, 1989, page 222.

9: In My Village

"everyone who believes in brotherhood": *The Josephine Baker Story*, 2000, page 266.

"she would have to prove": *The Josephine Baker Story*, 2000, page 268.

"They were rolling around": *The Josephine Baker Story*, 2000, page 269.

"Look what God": *Naked at the Feast*, 1981, page 268.

"to adopt five little": *Josephine: The Hungry Heart*, 1993, page 326.

"I suffered a lot": *Naked at the Feast*, 1981, page 269.

"I'll be fifty this year": *Josephine*, 1977, page 204.

"As I am leaving": *Naked at the Feast*, 1981, page 274.

10: Joséphine and Jo Split

"The Heart-Rending Drama": *Josephine: The Hungry Heart*, 1993, page 342.

"Having lost their natural parents": *Josephine*, 1977, page 212.

"I was lucky": *Josephine: The Hungry Heart*, 1993, page 473.

"Mara has rickets": "Josephine Baker Adopts Indian Boy," *The Age*, April 25, 1959.

"Banking on the theory": "Jo Baker Conquers New Paris as Old." *Washington Afro-American*, June 16, 1959.

"We feel it is our duty": "International Family of 11 'Living Dolls.'" *Sydney Morning Herald*, March 10, 1963.

"'We are not angry": Ollie Stewart. "Divorce for Josephine, Jo Bouillon?" *Baltimore Afro-American*, July 2, 1957.

"I didn't realize": Beverley Mitchell. "Singer's Brood Is International," *Montreal Gazette*, November 14, 1963.

"I am happy to": *Josephine: The Hungry Heart*, 1993, page 392.

"You are here on the eve": *Josephine: The Hungry Heart*, 1993, page 371.

"Our World is toppling": *Josephine Baker*, 1988, page 208.

"Don't be worried": *Josephine: The Hungry Heart*, 1993, page xix.

"I, too, need $400,000": *Naked at the Feast*, 1981, page 291.

"These youngsters will come": "Different Races Can't Live Together? Miss Baker Has Reason for Disbelief," *Gasden Times*, March 15, 1964.

"The older children": *Josephine*, 1977, page 270.

11: Losing Les Milandes

"When we left": *Josephine*, 1977, page 257.

"I will not leave": *Josephine: The Hungry Heart*, 1993, page 409.

"I'm not bitter": *Naked at the Feast*, 1981, page 295.

"It was here that": *Josephine*, 1977, page 262.

"I wonder if I could have": *Naked at the Feast*, 1981, page 296.

"I don't deserve": *Josephine Baker*, 1988, page 248.

"Dear Boys and Girls": *Naked at the Feast*, 1981, page 302.

"Don't be silly": *Naked at the Feast*, 1981, page 302.

"For fun, she would": *Naked at the Feast*, 1981, page 302.

"Nobody wants me": *Naked at the Feast*, 1981, page 303.

"I don't understand what": *The Josephine Baker Story*, 2000, page 306.

"I saw her use everybody": *The Josephine Baker Story*, 2000, page 309.

12: The Curtain Falls

"I have an image to maintain": *Naked at the Feast*, 1981, page 313.

"Nobody can take": *The Josephine Baker Story*, 2000, page 314.

"At this moment it": *Josephine: The Hungry Heart*, 1993, page 476.

"Tired? Young people": *Josephine*, 1977, page 290.

"I shall dance all my life": *Josephine Baker*, 1988, page 256.

"the most sensational": *Naked at the Feast*, 1981, page 104.

BIBLIOGRAPHY

Books

Baker, Jean-Claude and Chris Chase. *Josephine: The Hungry Heart*. New York: Random House, 1993.

Baker, Josephine and Jo Bouillon. *Josephine*. New York: Harper & Row, Publishers, 1977.

Brown, Jayna. *Babylon Girls: Black Women Performers and the Shaping of the Modern*. Durham, North Carolina: Duke University Press, 2009.

Hammond, Patrick and Brian O'Connor. *Josephine Baker*. Boston: Little, Brown and Company, 1988.

Haney, Lynn. *Naked at the Feast: A Biography of Josephine Baker*. New York: Dodd Mead, 1981.

Papich, Stephen. *Remembering Josephine*. Indianapolis: The Bobbs-Merrill Company, 1976.

Rose, Phyllis. *Jazz Cleopatra: Josephine Baker in Her Time*. New York: Doubleday, 1989.

Wood, Ean. *The Josephine Baker Story*. London: Sanctuary Publishing Limited, 2000.

Newspapers

"Different Races Can't Live Together? Miss Baker Has Reason for Disbelief." *Gasden Times*, March 15, 1964.

"International Family of 11 'Living Dolls.'" *Sydney Morning Herald*, March 10, 1963.

"Jo Baker Conquers New Paris as Old." *Washington Afro-American*, June 16, 1959.

"Josephine Baker Adopts Indian Boy." *The Age*, April 25, 1959.

"Josephine Baker, Black Dancer, Weds a Real Count." *Milwaukee Journal*, June 22, 1971.

Mitchell, Beverley. "Singer's Brood Is International." *Montreal Gazette,* November 14, 1963.

Stewart, Ollie. "Divorce for Josephine, Jo Bouillon?" *The Afro-American*, July 2, 1957.

"Stork Club Refused to Serve Her, Josephine Baker Claims." *Milwaukee Journal*, October 19, 1956.

Websites

Corinna, Nicole. "When Frida Kahlo Set Her Eyes on Josephine Baker." http://lifeofanartist.hubpages.com/hub/When-Frida-Kahlo-Set-Her-Eyes-on-Josephine-Baker

"Josephine Baker." Notable Black American Women. Gale. 1992. *Gale Biography in Context*. http://ic.galegroup.com/ic/bic1/ReferenceDetailsPage/ReferenceDetailsWindow?displayGroupName=Reference&disableHighlighting=true&proдId=BIC1&action=e&windowstate=normal&catId=&documentId=GALE%7CK1623000015&mode=view&userGroupName=gotitans&jsid=45c9bae18e81d0eadfc534d36f31056e.

"Josephine Baker." *Voguepedia* online. www.vogue.com/voguepedia/Josephine_Baker

"Josephine Baker." The Biography.com website. www
    .biography.com/people/josephine-baker-9195959.
    "Official Site of Josephine Baker." www.cmgww.com/stars
    /baker/about/biography.html.
Theile, Merlind. "Adopting the World: Josephine Baker's Rain-
    bow Tribe." Spiegel International   October 2, 2009. www
    .spiegel.de/international/zeitgeist/adopting-the-world
    -josephine-baker-s-rainbow-tribe-a-652613.html.

INDEX